DELTA FORCE®
BLACK HAWK DOWN™
PRIMA'S OFFICIAL STRATEGY GUIDE

Michael Knight

Prima Games
A Division of Random House, Inc.
3000 Lava Ridge Court
Roseville, CA 95661
1-800-733-3000
www.primagames.com

Associate Product Manager: Christy L. Curtis

Project Editor: Teli Hernandez

Editorial Assistant: Matt Sumpter

Acknowledgments

A big thanks goes to Paul Olshan at NovaLogic for all his help in writing this book, along with his colleagues Barry Feather and Wes Eckhart. They offered the kind of support an author dreams about. I also greatly appreciate the people at Prima Games who made this book a reality. Finally I offer hugs and kisses to my wife Trisa for supporting me during this project, and to my four children—Beth, Sarah, Connor, and Tanner—for their love and understanding as daddy is busy meeting deadlines.

This book is dedicated not only to those who served in Task Force Ranger, but to all the men and women of the United States armed forces.

ISBN: 0-7615-4082-2

Library of Congress Catalog Card Number: 2002112902

Printed in the United States of America

03 04 05 06 DD 10 9 8 7 6 5 4 3 2 1

CONTENTS

INTRODUCTION

I can still remember watching the news on television nearly 10 years ago and seeing very disturbing images. I cannot forget the look on the face of a captured American pilot whose image was spread throughout the news media—on television and on the cover of news magazines. American troops were in the northeast African country of Somalia to help distribute food and relieve the famine caused by drought and civil war. I didn't understand why our troops were being killed.

A few years later I read about the military action on the streets of Mogadishu in David H. Hack's book *Hazardous Duty*. This peaked my curiousity, so when Mark Bowden's book *Black Hawk Down* hit the shelves, I grabbed a copy and devoured it. What had happened to American troops astounded me. We were fighting a new type of war, different from the one I grew up expecting during the Cold War. So of course, when the movie based on Bowden's book was released, I was there the first day—and impressed with how well it portrayed the book and the events. Now the events in Somalia are part of my high school world history class during the unit on modern Africa.

When I first heard that NovaLogic was planning a game based on this event, I was very interested in the project. So when I was offered the opportunity to write the strategy guide for the game, I jumped at the chance. I was not disappointed. *Delta Force—Black Hawk Down* puts the player right in the middle of the conflict, and provides a realistic experience to gamers.

HOW TO USE THIS BOOK

The purpose of this book is to provide strategy and information to help you become a better player and advance through the missions successfully. The first chapter provides a historical background to the events portrayed in *Delta Force—Black Hawk Down*. Following that, "Chapter 2: The Arsenal" offers information on the various weapons and equipment you will use during the game. "Chapter 3: Basic Training" covers the game interface and how to play effectively while also adding tactics you can use throughout the game. The next section of the book, chapters 4 through 19, are walkthroughs for each of the campaign missions in the single-player game. In these chapters you will find a briefing, a list of what weapons to use, and step-by-step instructions on how to complete all your objectives and finish the mission alive. The final chapter, 20, covers the exciting multiplayer game. It discusses the different types of missions and how you can operate successfully with other players over the Internet or on a local area network (LAN).

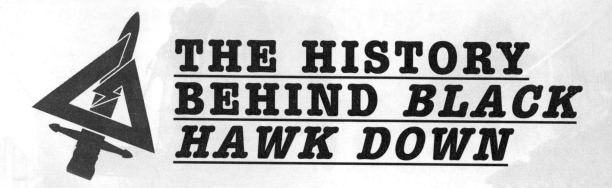

THE HISTORY BEHIND *BLACK HAWK DOWN*

UNREST AND STARVATION

The story of *Delta Force—Black Hawk Down* began in 1991 as the government of Somalia collapsed under civil war. Agriculture and business came to a halt as a majority of the men took up arms in the fight. A widespread drought furthered the devastation of the civil war by causing starvation throughout the country. Private relief organizations rushed food and other supplies to the hungry Somali people. By this time the country was under the control of rival clans led by warlords. These warlords demanded payments from the relief organizations and required that their clan distribute all food supplies. However, instead of distributing the food, the warlords kept it for themselves and used it to feed their supporters rather than the general population.

United Nations and U.S. Involvement

In response to the lawlessness and suffering of the Somali people, the United Nations Security Council adopted Resolution 751 in April, 1992, which established UNOSOM I, the first United Nations operation in Somalia. The purpose of the mission was to end hostilities so that humanitarian aid could be provided to the population. When it became apparent that UNOSOM I did not have the teeth to make a difference, the U.S. government began Operation Provide Relief. During the six months of this operation, 28,000 metric tons of supplies were airlifted into Somalia. By December of 1992 the lawlessness in the country, especially in the capital city of Mogadishu, made the distribution of the supplies to the people who needed it most impossible. As a result of the problems, President Bush initiated Operation Restore Hope.

This operation, led by U.S. military forces as part of an international coalition, was to exist until conditions stabilized to the point where it could be turned over to a UN peacekeeping force. U.S. forces were successful in their objectives; so in March of 1993, plans were made to turn over the mission to UNOSOM II. This UN peacekeeping force had three main objectives: disarm the warlord's clans, rebuild a government, and create a secure environment throughout the country. As a part of this mission, the United States provided a Quick Reaction Force (QRF) to operate under the U.S. Forces Somalia (USFORSOM). USFORSOM was assigned to use military force to secure areas so that humanitarian aid and the UNOSOM II objectives could be achieved. In other words, the U.S. forces were to keep areas safe so that peacekeepers could operate unmolested by the warlords.

The UN operation threatened the power of the clans, who referred to themselves as militias. Most opposed to the operation was the Somali National Alliance (SNA), the largest and most powerful militia led by Mohammed Farah Aidid. As the former Somali army Chief of Staff, Aidid could call on thousands of armed fighters equipped with rocket propelled grenades (RPGs), light artillery, and even a few tanks. To build up anti-U.S. and anti-UN sentiment, Aidid ran pirate radio broadcasts and organized demonstrations. In response to this, Turkish Lieutenant General Cevik Bir, commander of UNOSOM II, ordered the Pakistani Light Armor Brigade to shut down the radio station. However, sources in the UNOSOM headquarters informed Aidid of the raid. He put together an ambush that killed 24 Pakistani soldiers and wounded another 50.

The Gloves Come Off

The next day, the UN Security Council approved Resolution 837, which authorized "all necessary measures" to go after those responsible and bring them to trial. Both the UN and United States focused on Aidid's clan as an example to all others. If they could be controlled, the rest would fall into line. During a two-week period, the U.S. and UN forces seized Aidid's radio station, as well as his headquarters compound and home. However, the manhunt for Aidid continued and a $250,000 bounty was offered for his capture. Although the SNA backed off, it continued harassing the U.S. forces through mortar attacks against the U.S. QRF at Mogadishu airport.

To deal with the continued attacks by Aidid, the United States assembled Task Force Ranger (TFR). This force of 450 men comprised Squadron C, Delta Force; Bravo Company, 75th Ranger Regiment; and the 160th Special Operations Aviation Regiment, known as the "Nightstalkers," which provided MH-60 Black Hawk and AH-6J Little Bird helicopters for the force. Although TFR made several raids and captured key members of the SNA, they could not find Aidid. In response, Aidid's militia attacked UN and U.S. QRF forces. But what he really wanted was TFR. The U.S. commander requested armor to support his troops, but this request was denied out of fear of escalating the situation.

The Battle

On October 3, 1993, the U.S. commander learned of a meeting of the SNA's key leaders to be held later that afternoon at a building near the Olympic Hotel in Mogadishu's Bakara Market district. The plan was similar to other TFR operations. Four chalks (teams) of Rangers would fast rope out of the Black Hawks to form security teams which would seal off the area. Then the Little Birds would fly in and drop off about 40 Delta commandos, tasked with entering the building and grabbing the leaders. A ground convoy would arrive to pick up the prisoners, the Delta commandos, and the Rangers and take them back to the airfield.

Everything went fine until RPG attacks destroyed a five ton truck and Humvee. Aidid's militia assembled around TFR faster than expected. Within another five minutes, Super 61, one of the orbiting Black Hawks, was hit by an RPG and forced down 300 yards to the east. This was the moment Aidid was waiting for. He could never get at TFR before because of its mobility. However, a downed helicopter would hold them in place while thousands of militia surrounded TFR.

A reaction team on one of the airborne Black Hawks was ordered to the crash site, as was a part of the assault force. One of the Little Birds landed and recovered a couple of the survivors. Next, Rangers and U.S. Air Force Special Operations Forces of the reaction team fast roped from another Black Hawk. This helicopter was also struck by an RPG round as the team was nearly on the ground. However, the pilot was able to get the Black Hawk back to the airfield after dropping off the team.

The reaction team arrived in time to secure the crash site, where they were surrounded by hundreds of militia, in addition to women and children. The ground convoy was ordered to head for the crash site to pick up the men and bring them back to the airfield. However, after taking many attacks by rifle and RPG fire, in addition to becoming lost, the convoy was ordered to deliver the prisoners to the airfield to complete the objectives of the mission. Another rescue effort would be made.

Just as things seemed under control, a second Black Hawk, Super 64, was struck by an RPG and crashed about two miles from the objective building at about 1700 hours. While contingency plans allowed for a chopper to go down, two downed birds was thought to be almost impossible.

At the airfield, members of the QRF were assembled into a rescue force of 21 lightly armored vehicles. At 1745 hours, they rolled into Mogadishu and were quickly attacked by militia. The soldiers dismounted from their vehicles and fought back, firing approximately 60,000 rounds of ammunition in an attempt to drive away the SNA. At 1821 hours, they were ordered to the airfield, though it took them nearly an hour to break contact with the enemy.

With the only reaction team at the first crash site and the rescue convoy turned back, there was no other resource to assist at the second crash site. Therefore, Super 62, another Black Hawk orbiting the area, set down two Delta snipers at the crash site. Master Sergeant Gary Gordon and Sergeant First Class Randall Shughart took up positions to defend the crash site until help could arrive. Super 62 took off to provide air cover, but was hit by an RPG round. It crash-landed at the airfield, leaving the two Delta snipers on their own.

The snipers defended the pilot who survived the crash of Super 64 until each was mortally wounded. In addition to the defenders at the first crash site, 90 other TFR members were stranded in Mogadishu when night fell. Because they expected the raid to be a quick in-and-out affair like all the rest, the soldiers had left their night vision equipment at the base. They were also running out of medical supplies, water, and ammunition.

At 2330 hours, a convoy of 4 Pakistani tanks, 24 Malaysian armored personnel carriers (APCs), and infantry including 50 members of TFR who had returned with the prisoners, set out for the crash sites. They fought their way block-by-block and eventually divided into two columns; one headed to each crash site. At 0155 hours on October 4th, one column arrived at the first crash site and linked up with the defenders and remaining TFR soldiers. The second convoy arrived at the second crash site to find the snipers and Black Hawk crew missing. Both convoys then headed back to base, arriving at around 0530 hours.

Aftermath

Although the mission achieved its objectives, it resulted in 18 dead and 84 wounded Americans. A 19th American soldier was killed 2 days later in a mortar attack on the air base. Estimates place Somali casualties around 500 dead and thousands wounded. As a result of this battle, the U.S. QRF was reinforced with air and naval forces, tanks, and infantry fighting vehicles. However, President Clinton announced the intention to withdraw U.S. forces from Somalia by March 1994. A year after the United States withdrew, UNOSOM II pulled out with the assistance of U.S. military forces under the auspices of Operation United Shield. Mohammed Farah Aidid declared himself president of Somalia following the UN withdrawal. He died on August 1, 1996, as a result of complications due to gunshot wounds.

CONGRESSIONAL MEDALS OF HONOR

In recognition of their actions during the battle of October 3, 1993, the two Delta Force snipers who defended the second crash site were posthumously awarded the nations highest decoration, the Congressional Medal of Honor. Following are the citations for each soldier as found on the U.S. Army Center of Military History website (*www.army.mil/CMH-pg/Moh1.htm*).

Gordon, Gary I.

Rank and organization: Master Sergeant, U.S. Army

Place and date: 3 October 1993, Mogadishu, Somalia

Born: Lincoln, Maine

Citation

Master Sergeant Gordon, United States Army, distinguished himself by actions above and beyond the call of duty on 3 October 1993, while serving as Sniper Team Leader, United States Army Special Operations Command with Task Force Ranger in Mogadishu, Somalia. Master Sergeant Gordon's sniper team provided precision fires from the lead helicopter during an assault and at two helicopter crash sites, while subjected to intense automatic weapons and rocket propelled grenade fires. When Master Sergeant Gordon learned that ground forces were not immediately available to secure the second crash site, he and another sniper unhesitatingly volunteered to be inserted to protect the four critically wounded personnel, despite being well aware of the growing number of enemy personnel closing in on the site. After his third request to be inserted, Master Sergeant Gordon received permission to perform his volunteer mission. When debris and enemy ground fires at the site caused them to abort the first attempt, Master Sergeant Gordon was inserted one hundred meters south of the crash site. Equipped with only his sniper rifle and a pistol, Master Sergeant Gordon and his fellow sniper, while under intense small arms fire from the enemy, fought their way through a dense maze of shanties and shacks to reach the critically injured crew members. Master Sergeant Gordon immediately pulled the pilot and the other crew members from the aircraft, establishing a perimeter which placed him and his fellow sniper in the most vulnerable position. Master Sergeant Gordon used his long range rifle and side arm to kill an undetermined number of attackers until he depleted his ammunition. Master Sergeant Gordon then went back to the wreckage, recovering some of the crew's weapons and ammunition. Despite the fact that he was critically low on ammunition, he provided some of it to the dazed pilot and then radioed for help. Master Sergeant Gordon continued to travel the perimeter, protecting the downed crew. After his team member was fatally wounded and his own rifle ammunition exhausted, Master Sergeant Gordon returned to the wreckage, recovering a rifle with the last five rounds of ammunition and gave it to the pilot with the words, "good luck." Then, armed only with his pistol, Master Sergeant Gordon continued to fight until he was fatally wounded. His actions saved the pilot's life. Master Sergeant Gordon's extraordinary heroism and devotion to duty were in keeping with the highest standards of military service and reflect great credit upon him, his unit and the United States Army.

Shughart, Randall D.

Rank and organization: Sergeant First Class, U.S. Army

Place and date: 3 October 1993, Mogadishu, Somalia

Born: Newville, Pennsylvania

Citation

Sergeant First Class Shughart, United States Army, distinguished himself by actions above and beyond the call of duty on 3 October 1993, while serving as a Sniper Team Member, United States Army Special Operations Command with Task Force Ranger in Mogadishu, Somalia. Sergeant First Class Shughart provided precision sniper fires from the lead helicopter during an assault on a building and at two helicopter crash sites, while subjected to intense automatic weapons and rocket propelled grenade fires. While providing critical suppressive fires at the second crash site, Sergeant First Class Shughart and his team leader learned that ground forces were not immediately available to secure the site. Sergeant First Class Shughart and his team leader unhesitatingly volunteered to be inserted to protect the four critically wounded personnel, despite being well aware of the growing number of enemy personnel closing in on the site. After their third request to be inserted, Sergeant First Class Shughart and his team leader received permission to perform this volunteer mission. When debris and enemy ground fires at the site caused them to abort the first attempt, Sergeant First Class Shughart and his team leader were inserted one hundred meters south of the crash site. Equipped with only his sniper rifle and a pistol, Sergeant First Class Shughart and his team leader, while under intense small arms fire from the enemy, fought their way through a dense maze of shanties and shacks to reach the critically injured crew members. Sergeant First Class Shughart pulled the pilot and the other crew members from the aircraft, establishing a perimeter which placed him and his fellow sniper in the most vulnerable position. Sergeant First Class Shughart used his long range rifle and side arm to kill an undetermined number of attackers while traveling the perimeter, protecting the downed crew. Sergeant First Class Shughart continued his protective fire until he depleted his ammunition and was fatally wounded. His actions saved the pilot's life. Sergeant First Class Shughart's extraordinary heroism and devotion to duty were in keeping with the highest standards of military service and reflect great credit upon him, his unit and the United States Army.

THE ARSENAL

As you take the role of Army infantry, Ranger, or Delta Force operator, you have the ability to use a number of different weapons to help you accomplish your objectives. The different types of weapons and equipment you carry are divided into four main categories: primary weapons, secondary weapons, grenades, and accessories.

PRIMARY WEAPONS

Your primary weapon is what you will use extensively during a mission, so choose one that is suited to each particular mission. Primary weapons consist of assault rifles, sniper rifles, machineguns, and a submachine gun.

M16A2

Ammo Type: 5.56 x 45mm
Rounds per Clip: 30
Rounds Carried: 300

The M16A2 has been in wide use by the armies of more than 30 countries since its introduction to the U.S. Army in 1957. The A2 version is more accurate and durable than its Vietnam-era relatives. Heavier than the weapons carried by Delta Force and Rangers, the M16 has two firing modes: semiautomatic and three-round burst. The 10th Mountain Division and most standard Army units use it. It can be fitted with the M203 grenade launcher. The M16 offers only its standard iron sights when a scoped view is used.

CAR-15

Ammo Type: 5.56 x 45mm

Rounds per Clip: 30

Rounds Carried: 300

First used extensively in Vietnam, the CAR-15 soon became a standard rifle in the U.S. Army. It is lightweight, fully automatic, and more maneuverable than the M16, making it the preferred assault rifle of Delta Force. The only downside is that the shorter barrel reduces accuracy. The CAR-15 can be fired on full-automatic mode, although semiautomatic mode is preferable for long-range shooting. The accuracy is better and it also helps conserve ammunition. This assault rifle features reflex sights, which provide magnification during scoped view, increased accuracy, and improved peripheral vision as compared to standard scopes. In fact, when using a CAR-15, use the scoped view as much as possible.

M203 Grenade Launcher

Ammo Type: High-explosive grenades

Rounds per Clip: 1

Rounds Carried: 10

Mounted under the barrel of either an M16 or CAR-15, this single-shot, breach-loading launcher fires a 40mm low-velocity grenade round. This weapon gives a soldier a quick means of firing an explosive round at long range. The over-under configuration means that the soldier does not have to change weapons when a grenade launcher is needed. This weapon is great for putting grenades through windows and other limited openings. In addition, the rounds explode on impact. During missions, the M203 is best used against concentrations of enemies where a single round can cause a lot of damage, or against technicals and mounted-weapon positions.

MP5A3

Ammo Type: 9mm
Rounds per Clip: 30
Rounds Carried: 300

Primarily used by the 160th Special Operation's Aviation Regiment (SOAR) pilots as a personal side arm, the MP5 is currently the world's most popular submachine gun. It fires a 9mm round, which reduces its stopping power, but it is very accurate. The SD (Sound Dampened) variant, used by Delta Force, is fitted with a sound suppressor. The MP5 is the only silenced weapon in the arsenal. This allows it to be used during covert operations where your teams must avoid alerting others to their presence. The MP5 uses iron sights during scoped view and offers only fully automatic rate of fire. It is an excellent weapon for urban and Close-Quarters Battle (CQB) situations.

M21

Ammo Type: 7.62 x 51mm
Rounds per Clip: 20
Rounds Carried: 200
Rates of Magnification: 2x, 4x, 6x, 8x

This semiautomatic sniper rifle is fitted with a medium-power scope that is adjustable to allow for accurate sniping from helicopters or moving ground vehicles. Introduced in 1969 as the XM21, it was initially used in the Vietnam conflict as an upgrade from the M14. It was fielded with a hardwood stock and later replaced by fiberglass. The semiautomatic fire allows for faster target acquisition and firing, but sacrifices the accuracy of a bolt-action rifle. This is a good choice for a sniper who will engage several targets in quick succession, or may be engaged in closer-range combat than usual for a sniper.

M24

Ammo Type: 7.62 x 51mm

Rounds per Clip: 6

Rounds Carried: 180

Rates of Magnification: 2x, 4x, 6x, 8x, 10x, 12x, 14x

This bolt-action sniper weapon system has been a standard in the military since it was designed to replace the M21 by offering increased range and accuracy over its predecessors. For longer-range combat, the M24 is one of the best sniper rifles. It combines a large magazine and a good scope. However, because it is bolt-action, the sniper using it should refrain from close combat where a higher rate of fire is necessary.

MCRT .300 Tactical

Ammo Type: .300 Magnum

Rounds per Clip: 4

Rounds Carried: 180

Rates of Magnification: 2x, 4x, 6x, 8x, 10x, 12x, 14x, 16x, 18x

This McMillan bolt-action sniper weapon is chambered for the Winchester .300 magnum round, giving it excellent accuracy and damage upon impact. The MCRT also boasts one of the best accuracy ratings for all the sniper rifles. If you want to be a sniper, this is the weapon you will need. With the best scope available in the game, you can zoom between 2x and 18x magnification. The only downside to this rifle is that the magazine holds only four rounds.

Barrett M82A1

Ammo Type: .50 BMG

Rounds per Clip: 10

Rounds Carried: 100

Rates of Magnification: 2x, 4x, 6x, 8x, 10x, 12x

The Barrett M82A1 is considered an antimaterial weapon designed to stop armored personnel carriers and the like. Its .50-caliber bullet is effective against many light-skinned vehicles and structures. Its weight makes it extremely hard to deploy in traditional sniper missions, so it is not often used unless it will not have to be moved very much. The accuracy of the Barrett is limited only by the ammunition used. At the best of times, it boasts 1 MOA (Minute of Angle) accuracy and a range of 1,800 meters. This is one heavy rifle. Choose it only if you stay in one place. Its heavy-caliber round makes it an excellent choice for using against technicals and other vehicles at extreme ranges. However, for anti-personnel uses, you are better off selecting the MCRT.

M249 SAW

Ammo Type: 5.56mm

Rounds per Clip: 200

Rounds Carried: 600

The M249 SAW (Squad Automatic Weapon) has been a standard feature of the fire team since the 1980s. Its ability to lay down high amounts of reliable, accurate fire has made it indispensable. Typically, one SAW is issued per six-man team and requires only one soldier to operate. It is able to fire from 30-round M16 magazines or 200-round drum magazines utilizing belt-fed disintegrating metallic links. As a personal weapon, the SAW and any of the machineguns are not very useful. They are quite large and not as accurate during movement. They also do not have a scoped view. Instead, machineguns should be used as support weapons for a fire team, laying down cover and support fire for the rest of the team as they maneuver. The SAW's high rate of fire can easily create a kill zone in any open area such as a courtyard or street. This weapon is best used from a prone position. If you need a machinegun, the SAW is your best choice.

M60E3

Ammo Type: 7.62 x 51mm

Rounds per Clip: 200

Rounds Carried: 600

The M60 gas-powered machinegun is a larger and more powerful weapon than the M249. It fires the 7.62 round for increased range and stopping power, but its heavier weight and ammunition make the M60 awkward to fire unless the bipod is used. The M60 also features a replaceable barrel to prevent overheating.

M240

Ammo Type: 7.62 x 51mm

Rounds per Clip: 200

Rounds Carried: 600

The M240 is a standard machinegun in many North Atlantic Treaty Organization (NATO) countries, where it is called the FN MAG-58. The M240 is often vehicle-mounted with a twin handle and thumb-actuated trigger. For handheld use, a rifle stock and standard trigger mechanism are used. There is no selective fire on the M240; it can be used only for fully automatic fire. The M240 is one of the most reliable machineguns in use today.

SECONDARY WEAPONS

Secondary weapons are usually considered backup weapons, used if something happens to your primary weapon or you run out of ammo for it. Consisting of pistols or a shotgun, these weapons have a limited amount of ammunition. They are also meant to be used at closer range than primary weapons.

Beretta M9

Ammo Type: 9mm

Rounds per Clip: 15

Rounds Carried: 30

The M9 is the standard sidearm of the U.S. Army. Used by the Rangers, the higher-capacity magazine and increased accuracy during rapid fire makes this weapon more manageable than the Colt .45. This should be your standard secondary weapon during most missions.

Colt M1911A1 .45

Ammo Type: .45 automatic

Rounds per Clip: 7

Rounds Carried: 28

A high-powered sidearm preferred by Delta Operators for its reliability and stopping power, the Colt .45 has armed the United States military since 1911. The design was standardized in 1926 and remains unchanged. The pistol is extremely accurate when used for single shots. With a smaller magazine capacity, the .45 needs reloading more often. However, its heavier round drops an enemy with a single hit.

Remington 780 Shotgun

Ammo Type: 12-gauge 00 buckshot

Rounds per Clip: 7

Rounds Carried: 14

Used for breaching doors and extreme close-quarters combat, this 12-gauge has high stopping power in close, but loses force with range. It is not very accurate, but provides good coverage close in. Delta Operators usually replace the stock with a pistol grip and shorten the barrel to make it easier to carry as a secondary weapon. Since it comes with only 14 shots, the shotgun has limited usefulness during a mission. However, it is excellent when clearing a building, because a single shot takes out several enemies if they are close together. This makes the shotgun effective, especially if ammo boxes are available along the way.

GRENADES

Grenades are hand-thrown explosives that are used to kill, stun, or conceal. During most campaign missions, you carry five of each. However, during multiplayer games the number and type of grenades carried will vary depending on your specialty.

M67 Fragmentation Grenade

When thrown, the delayed fuse inside the M67 detonates 6.5 ounces of high explosive. The resulting high-velocity shrapnel can cause casualties out to 15 meters. Frag grenades are best used against concentrations of enemies or for attacking around corners. Because of the delayed fuse, you can bounce them off a wall or throw them over an obstacle, allowing you to take out an enemy without exposing yourself to fire. They are great for clearing a room. However, use caution, a frag grenade can kill your teammates—even you—if it detonates too close to you.

XM84 Stun Grenade

The XM84 "flashbang" is specifically designed to disorient and distract hostile forces in a non-lethal manner. The grenade produces a blinding flash of light and a noise that temporarily confuses anyone in its immediate area. While the frag grenade may seem a better option than a flashbang because of its lethality, the flashbang affects a larger area. When it detonates, people nearby are incapable of putting up any resistance. Therefore, throwing one into a room or area before entering allows you to rush into a room without worrying about taking enemy fire. You can then neutralize all hostiles before they recover, if necessary. Flashbangs are also useful for suppressing hostiles in a room with civilians or hostages whom you do not want to harm. When giving your team the order to enter and clear a room ("takedown"), they will automatically throw a flashbang into the room before entering.

AN-M8 HC Smoke Grenade

This grenade produces large clouds of thick, opaque, white smoke. It can be used to prevent line-of-sight during movement or to mark a location for fire-support or rescue teams. If you must cross a street that the enemy has set up as a kill zone, throw a smoke grenade or two between the enemy and where you must move through. This creates a temporary source of concealment allowing you to move unmolested.

ACCESSORIES

In addition to weapons, each soldier carries other equipment. For some missions, you can select from the first three accessories. For others, in which an accessory is necessary for the completion of an objective, it will be selected for you. Night-vision goggles and knives are always issued.

AT4

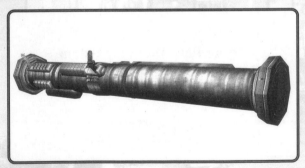

Ammo Type: Anti-tank rocket
Rounds Carried: 1

A light anti-armor rocket, the AT4 is a portable, shoulder-fired rocket launcher. Firing an 84mm unguided rocket, the AT4 is capable of penetrating 400mm of rolled homogeneous armor. Not only is the AT4 good for attacking armored vehicles, it can also be used against boats and mounted-weapons positions.

Satchel Charges

Ammo Type: C4

Satchels Carried: 2

A satchel charge is merely a container of C4 plastic explosive. It can be placed near a target, then set off by remote detonator. Move away from the charge before detonation. Satchel charges are useful for clearing roadblocks, destroying weapons systems, and blowing up bridges, small buildings, and other structures.

Claymores

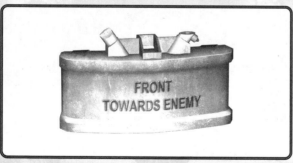

Ammo Type: Directional mine

Mines Carried: 4

Claymores are strictly anti-personnel. Because they are directional, face in the direction you want the blast to travel when placing them. These mines are extremely effective for defense and for covering narrow accessways, such as alleys. As with satchel charges, use the remote detonator to set off Claymores.

Night-Vision Goggles

Every soldier and operator is equipped with night-vision goggles during a mission. When activated, they allow the user to see in the dark by magnifying the ambient light. Although you use night-vision goggles during night missions, they are also extremely useful during daylight missions in which you must operate indoors where shadows and dark rooms hide enemies. The only problems with night-vision goggles are the monochrome view and the limited depth of field. For long-range targeting, you are best off using the existing light rather than the night-vision goggles. The goggles can also be used with binoculars and weapons scopes.

Knife

Every soldier is issued a combat knife for use during a mission. This weapon is for extremely close range. It is silent and kills with one attack. However, because most of the enemies you face carry firearms, avoid using this weapon except when absolutely necessary—such as when you run out of ammo.

BASIC TRAINING

Listen up! In *Delta Force—Black Hawk Down*, you are put right into the action with the first mission. Somalia is a combat zone, and you must be ready to fight as soon as you arrive. Therefore, this chapter on Basic Training has been provided for you to review on your flight to northeastern Africa. If you have been involved in other operations around the world (in other games), you may be familiar with some of the material. It is still a good idea to review the basics, but it is vital that you become familiar with the specifics of combat in Somalia, because every operation is different. Pay attention and read carefully so your trip home isn't in a body bag.

THE INTERFACE

Delta Force—Black Hawk Down is similar to other first-person shooters you may have played. Depending on your experience, you may find this game a bit more intense; taking fire from every direction imaginable while moving through Mogadishu can really draw you into the game.

Getting Started

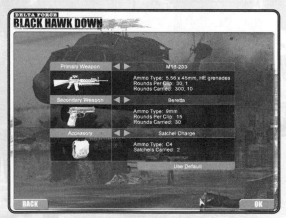

When you first are assigned a single-player mission in the campaign, or select one from the missions you have already completed, you will receive a short description of the mission. You are shown the default loadout of weapons and equipment you will carry. The default loadout contains what you need for the mission. If this is your first time playing the mission, you don't know what you'll be up against, so take the default loadout.

Although the default kit is usually good to take your first time through a mission, you can customize it to suit your style of play.

Later, if you play the mission subsequent times, feel free to experiment with different combinations of primary weapons, secondary weapons, and explosives. For some missions, you will not be able to select a different type of explosive; this is because you need a specific type in order to complete one or more of the objectives during the mission. Also, not all primary weapons may be available to you during all missions. This is usually limited by the unit with which you are serving for that mission, or by other restrictions.

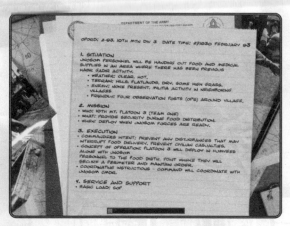

Read through the briefing to get your initial orders and see what you are up against.

After you receive information on the mission and have selected your loadout, prepare to begin the mission. While you wait for the mission to load, read the briefing provided on the load screen. Don't feel rushed. The game waits after loading for you to press a key or click the mouse to actually enter the mission. Each briefing provides information on the mission, including the Situation, Mission, and Execution.

The Situation lists the basic purpose of the mission along with weather, terrain, types, and numbers of enemies you might be facing, and whether friendly units operate in the area.

The Mission part of the briefing lists the units involved in the specific mission, the main focus of the mission, and when it will start.

Finally, the Execution part provides more detailed instructions on how the mission should be carried out.

In the Mission—the Game Screen

After the briefing, you get into the mission itself. The game screen is set up in first-person so you see what your character sees. At the bottom center of the screen is your current weapon held at the ready. The screen also features a Heads-Up Display (HUD). This HUD places information right on the screen for easy access during a mission. It consists of the Global Positioning System (GPS) map and Character Information.

The game screen's Heads-Up Display (HUD) provides important information during a mission.

GPS Map

To the right of your weapon is the GPS map. This instrument gives you a top-down view of the Area of Operations (AO) with the position of your character directly in the center. A compass heading with the letter "N" indicates north. On the GPS map, 12 o'clock is always the direction you are facing. Therefore, if you want to head north, turn until "N" is at 12 o'clock. You can also zoom the GPS view in and out by pressing ⊟ or ⊡.

The GPS map includes a couple of other useful features. During missions, you are ordered to move through various waypoints. These waypoints appear on the GPS map as lines that show the direction to the next waypoint. You do not have to walk that straight line on your way through the mission's waypoints. The line just helps point you in the right direction. As discussed later in the tactics section of this chapter, you should hug the walls of buildings or zigzag through alleys rather than take a direct course out in the open. Directly below the GPS map is a readout listing your next waypoint, the distance to that waypoint, and the current map grid coordinates for your location.

TIP *The GPS map even informs you if your next waypoint is on an upper or lower level. Look at the little shape on the left side. If it is a circle, the waypoint is at the same level as your character's current position. A triangle pointing either up or down signifies upper level or lower level, respectively—very useful when operating in multi-story buildings.*

At times during a mission, you will take fire and not know from where. This is especially true for urban operations where enemies could be firing at you from every alley and upstairs window near your position. To help locate the direction of threats, the GPS map also includes an indicator illustrating the direction of enemy fire. Yellow sectors indicate the direction of any enemy fire. If red sectors appear, they indicate the direction of fire that is hitting you! Whenever you hear gunshots, take a quick look down at your GPS map to see where it is originating. Then maneuver or take action accordingly so those yellow sectors do not become red.

Character Information

In the bottom-left corner of the screen is information about the character you control. It contains an icon of a soldier and a weapons box.

The character icon illustrates two types of information: the health of your character and his posture. Health is shown by color. If your icon is green, you are healthy. Yellow means that your soldier is lightly wounded, and red indicates more serious wounds. Posture is shown as standing, crouching, or prone.

Below the icon is the weapons box, which shows your currently selected weapon and its firing mode. Below this box, you can see how much ammo remains in the current magazine and how much total ammo you have on your person.

Mission Objectives

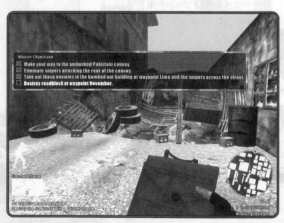

During the course of a mission you are given various objectives to complete. You can bring up a window displaying your current objectives by pressing [tab]. Press this key again to hide the window. The objectives for the mission are listed in order with a check box to the left of each objective. Once an objective is completed, a red X appears in the box.

Press [tab] to bring up mission objectives.

TIP *Press [G] during a mission to bring up your mission briefing.*

Map Screen

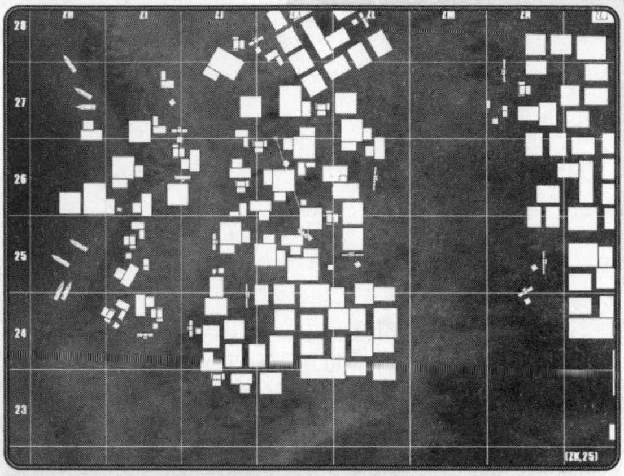

Use the map to navigate around your AO.

Although the GPS map can give you a quick look at your surroundings, the map screen is much more useful for planning your advance or coordinating with other team members during multiplayer games. Press [M] to open a small quarter-screen map. Press it again to open a full-screen view of the map. A third press closes the map screen. Unlike in the GPS map, the orientation of the map does not change as you turn. Instead, north is always at the top of the map. Waypoint lines are still shown on all maps, as are topographical and structural features such as rivers, hills, and buildings.

Looking Around—Different Views of the Action

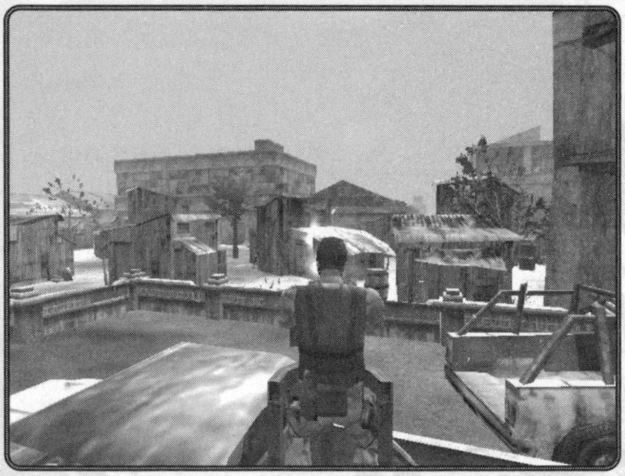

A third-person view can be helpful at times.

At times it can be useful to get a different view of the situation. The standard view of the game is first-person with your weapon displayed on the screen. However, you can get rid of the weapon in the view by pressing [F1]. To return to the view with the weapon, press [F3]. A third-person view can be selected by pressing [F4]. From this view, you can use the number pad keys to adjust this camera view even further; [8], [2], [4], and [6] pan the view up, down, left, and right, respectively; [7] and [9] zoom the view in and out; [5] returns the camera to the default view. You can sometimes use the third-person view to see what is around a corner without exposing yourself to enemy fire. Just be careful to use this view only when your character is in a relatively safe position, because it is very difficult to shoot from this view.

CONTROLLING YOUR CHARACTER

If you have ever played a first-person shooter game, you should have no trouble with the controls. On the other hand, if you are new to this type of game, don't worry, the controls are very easy to pick up. The game uses a combination of the keyboard and mouse to control your character. Whether rookie or veteran, you should check out the following section to get a good idea of how to effectively control your character.

Movement

Movement is simple. The mouse controls which direction your character faces and moves. By moving the mouse around, you cause your character to look up, down, left, and right. *Delta Force—Black Hawk Down* uses what is commonly known as the "WSAD" keyboard configuration for movement. W and S move your character forward and backward. Turning or changing direction is controlled by the mouse. A and D cause your character to sidestep left and right. This is referred to as strafing. When strafing, the character continues to face in the same direction while moving laterally.

Peeking

At times, you will want to look around a corner or through a doorway without exposing your entire body. By pressing either Q or E, you can cause your character to lean past a corner so he can see and fire while only offering the enemy a small target. You will use this type of action quite a bit during urban operations.

Peeking is much safer than running around a corner.

Stance

Your character can assume three different stances. The default is standing ([C]). While standing, your character can run, but this posture offers the largest target to the enemy. Pressing [X] causes your character to drop to a crouch. While he cannot move as quickly, your character is more stable while firing and offers a smaller target for the enemy. To drop prone, press [Z]. This is the most stable stance and offers the enemy the smallest target. However, movement is extremely slow because you must crawl around.

Most rookies never even use the stance feature of the game. They just run around everywhere and offer juicy targets to the enemy. As a general rule, whenever you stop movement to fire or look ahead, always drop to a crouch. This is what the real Delta Operators do, and If you want to survive in the game, you should too. If you are a sniper, find a good spot and drop prone. With some good cover or concealment, you can be nearly impossible for the enemy to locate and engage.

TIP *You can use the arrow keys rather than the WSAD configuration to control movement.*

COMBAT

Although moving around may be exciting in the beginning, it is only a tool for the real purpose of the game: moving your character into position to use your weapons. Let's take a look at what you need to do to become an effective and accurate marksman.

Firearms

A Humvee-mounted machinegun is just one of the powerful weapons you get to use.

For a majority of the time, you will use firearms. These can be assault rifles, sniper rifles, light machineguns, a submachine gun, pistols, or even a shotgun. To fire a weapon, all you have to do is left-click the mouse or press ⏎. When the ammo in the magazine or clip gets low, press R to reload. You can also take control of larger weapons positioned at various locations or mounted aboard helicopters or ground vehicles. In order to cycle through the various weapons and equipment you carry, you can either use the mousewheel or ↑ and ↓. Alternatively, you can press one of the number keys, 1 through 8, to choose a weapon or other item directly.

Weapons Accuracy

A scope view is much more accurate for shooting at distances rather than close range.

For each firearm, a targeting reticle appears in the center of the screen. However, just because the reticle is over a target does not mean that the bullet will hit it. This just provides a means of aiming your weapon. Where the bullets actually hit depends on a number of factors. In *Delta Force—Black Hawk Down*, weapon accuracy is modeled after real-life and common sense. You are more accurate when stationary and stable than when running. The less accurate your firing, the larger the circle of spread, or area, in which your bullets will hit. Therefore, even if you have the reticle centered on your target, if your spread area is larger than the target, you may miss the target altogether.

One of the best ways to improve accuracy (in addition to firing while motionless) is to use the scope view. For assault rifles and submachine guns, right-clicking the mouse or pressing 7 brings up a view with the weapons sight centered on the screen. This provides a bit of magnification and cuts down on your peripheral vision somewhat. However, it increases your accuracy because you are essentially looking down the barrel of the weapon rather than firing from the hip. Although you can move around with the scope view up at all times, it is usually best to bring up the scope view only when you need to fire at a target. This is especially true when you must fire quickly to get the drop on an enemy.

TIP *With the reflex sight on the CAR-15, you can actually use the scope view much more often because it does not block your view much. In fact, this sight was designed for Operators to use during close-quarters battle.*

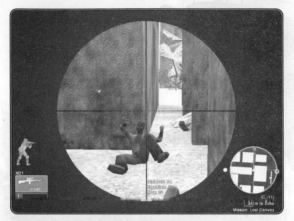

The sniper rifles allow you to take out enemies before they even know you are there.

Sniper rifles are equipped with a scope as well. When you bring up scope view, you are looking only through the scope. All peripheral vision is completely blocked. Each scope can cycle through magnification levels by using the mousewheel or ⌷ and ⌷. The scope makes your shots much more accurate and allows you to engage targets at long range. Each scope is also equipped with an automatic rangefinder. It will display in the scope view the distance to the target under the crosshairs. Then it will automatically set the elevation of the scope so that when you fire, your bullet will hit squarely on the spot where you were aiming.

At times, you will want to set the elevation manually. For example, if you are trying to hit a moving target, you will need to lead it or actually shoot ahead of it so that after the bullet travels the distance, it arrives where the target will be. Unfortunately, when using the automatic elevation, you are firing at a range of the object behind the target (where the crosshairs are) rather than at the range of the target itself. Therefore, place the crosshairs over the target to get the range. Then press ⌷ or ⌷+⌷ to cycle through various range setting for elevation. Now you can fire ahead of the target and have the correct elevation for the shot. This becomes more important for long- and very long-range shots where the time required for the bullet to reach the target is considerable.

Grenades

A flashbang may not kill, but is very useful.

Chapter 2 discussed the various types of grenades and when they should be used. However, here is where you learn how to throw them. Don't worry, it is a lot easier than sniping. To throw a grenade, aim in the direction you want to throw it and click the mouse. To give it a higher trajectory, look up as you throw it. For more control over the distance of your throw, hold the right mouse button to bring up a power meter. As you continue to hold down the button, the power meter will rise from 0 to 100 percent. Releasing the button causes you to throw the grenade at the power level displayed at the time of release. This allows you to just toss a grenade gently around a corner, bank it off a wall, or throw it hard for maximum distance. With a little bit of practice, you will be able to put a grenade wherever you want it to go.

Explosives

Explosives are a bit different. The AT4 functions just like a firearm. Just aim and shoot. It is a one-shot weapon. Once you fire it, there is no reloading. Until you pick up a box of ammo, that is all you get.

A satchel charge in the right place can clear a roadblock or other obstacle.

Satchel charges are dropped by your character by clicking the mouse. They stay put until detonated, which is accomplished by selecting the radio detonator and clicking the mouse as if to fire a weapon. If more than one charge is placed, the detonator sets off all the charges at the same time.

Claymores function a bit differently. Once you drop them, they act on their own, functioning like a proximity mine. When an enemy approaches a Claymore, it will self-detonate. Claymores are directional explosives, causing damage in the direction they face. When you place a Claymore, face the direction you want the blast to go, then click the mouse to drop the Claymore.

COMMANDING YOUR TEAM

During several missions, you are a leader of up to three other Rangers or Delta Operators. If there are more than two in your team, including yourself, the soldiers will be divided into two fireteams. You always lead Fireteam One. While the soldiers in your team will always follow you and engage enemies on their own, here are some special orders you can give.

Use the teammate commands to give orders to your team.

Special Orders

Key	Order
1	Auto Area Takedown
2	Hold Fire / Fire At Will—All
3	Hold Fire / Fire At Will—Fireteam Two
4	Hold Position / Follow Me—All
5	Hold Position / Follow Me—Fireteam Two
6	Team Spacing—2, 5, or 10 Meters
7	Throw Flashbang
8	Throw Frag Grenade

The Auto Area Takedown order is only available at some locations where your team is stacked up outside of a room. When this is available, a Takedown icon will appear on the game screen. Pressing `backspace` at this time also orders your team to take down a room. When you issue this order, one of your team will throw a flashbang into the room. The team will enter and clear the room as soon as the flashbang detonates.

The only time you want to use the Hold Fire orders are when you want to avoid detection by the enemy. Even if you issue this order, your team will still fire back at enemies who are attacking them.

The Hold Position order is great if you want your team, or part of your team, to stay back while you move forward. You can also leave Fireteam Two behind to cover your rear or flank while you maneuver around a position.

Team Spacing requires two keystrokes; the second sets the distance. For indoor operations, you usually want to keep your team in close. For outdoor ops, spread them out.

When you give an order to throw a grenade, one team member will try to throw a grenade to the point where *your reticle* is positioned. If you want the grenade thrown inside a room or building, be sure you have the door opened first.

Although you do not have to use any of these team commands, they can make your missions much more effective and enjoyable. Play around with the orders and use those that you like. The grenade orders can be a great way to use grenades while you keep your weapon at the ready in case an enemy appears ready to shoot you. Because someone else in your team is throwing the grenade, you are free to immediately deal with the enemy.

TACTICS

Chapters 4 through 19 cover the specific tactics you need to complete each of the missions in the campaign, but you should be familiar with a few general tactics. Let's take a look at them. They could save your virtual life and help you complete your objectives.

Cover and Concealment

Narrow alleys provide cover on two sides.

One of the most important tactics for staying alive is to prevent the enemy from being able to attack you. This is where cover and concealment come in. Cover is any obstacle that blocks an enemy's line of fire. In other words, it is something that will stop a bullet, such as a wall or building. Concealment, on the other hand, only blocks an enemy's line of sight. This could be provided by any object that hides you from the enemy's sight. For example, lying prone in high grass is concealment. The enemy cannot see you, but they could shoot in your direction and hit you.

Now that you understand the definition of these tactics, how do you use them? First, always have cover in mind. Most of the missions take place in urban terrain. That means buildings and walls. Do your best to move through alleys as much as possible, because both of your flanks are covered by the walls of the alley. If you have to move through an open area, rather than running straight across, try to move around the perimeter with a wall on one of your shoulders. The key is to minimize the number of directions from which the enemy can fire at you.

At times, you must cross a street or open area. Before you do, look to see if you can find any cover or concealment along the way. This could be some crates, a shack, or even a vehicle. Then locate a source of cover at the other end of your movement. With these in mind, run as fast as you can from one place of cover to the next. The last thing you want to do is stop out in the open and start shooting back. If you cannot find cover, then look for concealment; the enemy usually will not shoot at what it cannot see.

Take Your Time

There is an old saying that haste makes waste. This applies to combat as well. If you rush around during a mission, the only thing that will happen quickly is your death. None of the missions have a time limit. Therefore, there is no need to sprint around the map. Instead, take it slowly. Most missions provide waypoints with lines showing you the direction to the next waypoint. Do not think that you must follow the line. Instead, open up your map and plan how you will get there, taking advantage of cover and concealment as much as possible.

Look Ahead

From a safe, covered spot, scout the area ahead and clear it out as much as possible.

Along the same lines as taking your time is looking ahead. Before you go anywhere, take out your binoculars and scout the area you will be moving through. Look to see if there are any enemies patrolling or snipers in upstairs windows waiting to take a shot at you. Once you have spotted the enemies, fire at them from your position of cover so you can clear your path while minimizing your exposure. This also includes peeking. Never run around a corner. Peek around it to make sure it is clear. If not, you can take a shot or throw a grenade to clear it.

Engage at Long Range

Use binoculars to help line up a shot at distant enemies if you do not have a sniper rifle.

The best way to fight is to take out your enemy before he sees you. Try to engage enemies with long-range fire so you can take them out before they even know you are in the area. You do not have to use a sniper rifle to do this. Instead, you can use the binoculars to locate distant enemies and partially line up your shot. Then switch to scope view for your weapon and fire. Use the binoculars again to see if you get a hit.

Fire Discipline

While it may seem like fun to let loose with automatic fire or three-round bursts, unless at close range, you are best off keeping your primary weapon set at semiautomatic fire. Not only does this save ammo, but it also makes your shots more accurate. You can also use this tactic when using light machineguns or the CAR-15 in full-automatic mode. Fire quick bursts to improve accuracy. After about three rounds, the spread area is quite large for a weapon firing on full-automatic mode. Try firing two quick shots when using a weapon on semiautomatic to make sure you take down an enemy. In fact, with the M16, this is often preferable to three-round burst mode. Delta Operators refer to this as the "double tap."

Own the Night

Some missions take place at night or in low-light conditions. You always have night-vision goggles as part of your personal equipment. Use them. Even during the middle of the day, some buildings can be quite dark inside, allowing enemies to hide in the shadows and ambush you. Activate your goggles regularly when faced with these conditions. They can also be useful while outside in the daylight to see an enemy sniper hiding in the shadows of an upstairs window.

In some night missions, it can be nearly impossible to see anything without night-vision goggles. The enemy has the same limitations, but has no goggles. Therefore, you can move about with stealth and not be seen—as long as you avoid sources of light. Avoid fire barrels or other objects that light up the surrounding area and allow the enemy to see you. Also, when you fire your weapon in the dark, the enemy can see the muzzle flash and detect your presence.

Taking Down a Room

One of the toughest tactics to master is the room takedown. However, it is really pretty simple if you do it right. The first step is to wait for your team to stack up behind you. Make sure that team spacing is set to two meters and not a greater distance. Position yourself to one side of a doorway that you will use to enter the room. When everyone in your team is in position, throw a flashbang into the room and quickly switch back to your primary weapon.

When the Takedown icon appears, you can order your team to make an automatic takedown of a room.

When the flashbang detonates, rush into the room. If you are the first in, move along the closest wall to the far corner as you fire at the enemies stunned by the grenade. By hugging a wall, you help prevent enemies from hitting you from that side and avoid being shot by your team behind you as they go after the enemies. Also, the enemies around the perimeter of the room are less likely to be stunned than those in the middle who might have been closer to the grenade. By moving around the perimeter, you will engage these enemies first.

MARKA BREAKDOWN

BRIEFING

OPORD: 1-93, 10th Mtn. Div. 3

Date Time: 161530 February 93

1. Situation

A UN convoy was delivering food and medical supplies near the village of Marka when one of their trucks broke down, halting the convoy. Bandits are converging on the area in an attempt to steal the supplies.

- **Weather: Clear, hot.**
- **Terrain: Hills, flatlands, dry, some high grass.**
- **Enemy: Vehicles with mounted .50-caliber weapons (technicals), approx. 60 militia with small caliber weapons.**
- **Friendly: Aerial recon Black Hawk Golf Three.**

2. Mission

- **Who: 10th Mtn. Platoon 3—Victor Three.**
- **What: Provide security until convoy reaches town of Quorley.**
- **When: Immediately after briefing.**

3. Execution

- **Commander's Intent: Protect UN food/supply convoy from capture.**
- **Concept of Operation: Platoon 3 will deploy via Humvees to the location of the UN convoy. They will provide fire support until the column is ready to move.**
- **Coordinating Instructions: Golf Three is in the area if air support is needed.**

4. Service and Support

- **Basic Load: M21, Beretta, AT4.**

39

Summary of Mission

Ride shotgun aboard a Humvee and proceed to the Jubba Valley north of Marka, where a UN convoy of food and supplies has broken down. It is suspected the militia members might raid the convoy and take the shipment for themselves. Prevent this and escort the convoy to its destination.

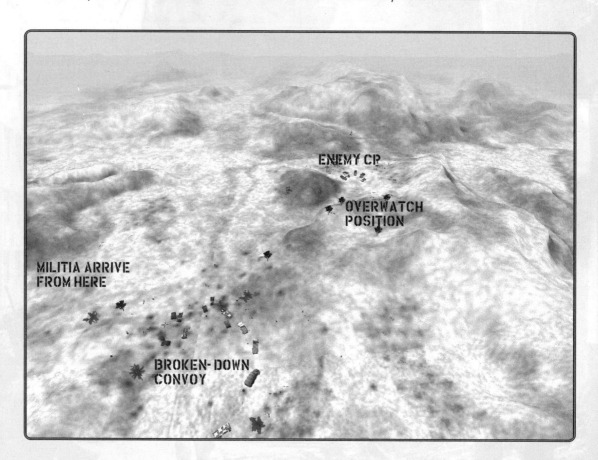

During most of the mission, you are going along for the ride in either a Humvee or a Black Hawk. However, in the middle of the mission, you must defend the broken-down convoy and assault an enemy command post.

Suggested Loadout

Primary Weapon: M21

Secondary Weapon: Beretta

Accessory: AT4

NOTE *During this mission, you can become acquainted with a variety of weapons systems. In addition to the personal weapons you carry, you will man a .50-caliber machinegun on a Humvee and a minigun on a Black Hawk helicopter. Don't worry about targets for your weapons; there are plenty to go around.*

TACTICS

1. Protect relief convoy with .50 cal MG.

You begin ready to rock-n-roll.

You begin the mission in a small village. A UN convoy has broken down and needs assistance. Your squad is being sent to escort it and ensure that it reaches its destination. You already begin aboard a Humvee behind a machinegun. Just stay put for now. You don't want to dismount and then get left behind.

Take out the militia trucks when you see them.

After the rest of the troops are ready, the patrol of Humvees moves out. You are exposed, so be careful. A short distance from the village, your patrol is ambushed by militia. Let 'em have it with the .50 caliber. Gunmen come at you from the right and from behind you. Take them out as soon as possible. Keep the gun rockin' and rollin' as you take out enemies on both sides of the road. Watch for technicals and militia with rocket-propelled grenades (RPGs); both can damage the Humvees. As you move past the ridges on both sides, watch for enemies firing down on you. A couple trucks appear to your left, so be ready. Scan back and forth to cover both sides of the road.

More trucks come from the left side.

TIP *It is difficult to keep the machinegun on a target while you move. Instead, aim at the correct elevation and behind the target while you fire. The motion of the Humvee will "walk" your fire onto the target.*

You'll arrive at the site where the convoy is being repaired. Stay in the Humvee for now and deal with the trucks headed in from the right and the militia on foot. Don't hit your own soldiers or vehicles. Your leader calls in air support to assist. Shortly thereafter, a Black Hawk flies over.

You have reached the convoy. Fire at the enemy approaching from the northwest.

2. Dismount and meet up with your teammates.

3. Follow teammates to enemy command post.

4. Eliminate resistance at enemy command post.

Follow these soldiers up the hill and over to the enemy CP.

Use the sniper rifle to take out enemies at long range. The enemy manning the machinegun on the technical is your first target.

Before the Black Hawk can land, you must clear the area. An enemy CP is nearby. Dismount from the Humvee and link up with a group of soldiers on foot to take it out. Follow them up the hill and along the ridge to the enemy site. The enemy is gathered around some vehicles. Because you have the high ground, fire down on them to clear out the CP and surrounding area. Drop prone or crouch while clearing out the CP or you will take some hits. If you shoot at the barrels, they blow up taking out any nearby enemies. More militia will appear from the back of the CP as well. Also, look out for enemies across the flat area firing at you from the trees and brush. Zoom in the scope view of the sniper rifle to take out these long-range targets.

5. Board helo and man left minigun.

6. Protect the convoy from the air.

When the CP is clear, the Black Hawk touches down.

Cover the convoy from the air.

When the area is clear, the Black Hawk comes in to land. Head over to it and hop aboard. Take control of the minigun on the left side and get ready for a lot of shooting. The pilot takes off and flies in front of the convoy, allowing you to clear any opposition.

A good tactic is to aim toward the front of the helicopter and track targets as you see them. The minigun makes short work of militia and vehicles alike. Technicals and trucks are your priorities because they have the heavier weaponry. Militia with the RPGs are easy to identify once they have fired a round; just follow the smoke trail back to the enemy.

Several militia scattered about the area are waiting to shoot at you.

Scratch another technical.

Be careful where you shoot. Sometimes the technicals drive up alongside the convoy.

As the Black Hawk orbits the area, take out as many enemies as you can locate. Eventually, the convoy begins moving again. As you fly over it, don't hit the vehicles in the convoy as you fire at enemies. Take care of the bandits on the road, then fly over Quorley. The town is clear, but a technical approaches from the opposite side. Take it out as you fly by, then provide aerial cover as the convoy arrives in the town. Once they are safe and secure, you receive orders to return to base.

The convoy has arrived safely. Mission accomplished.

Congratulations. You have successfully completed your mission.

BANDIT'S CROSSING

BRIEFING

OPORD: 2-93, 10th Mtn. Div. 3

Date Time: 271930 February 93

1. Situation

UNOSOM personnel will be handing out food and medical supplies in an area where there has been previous Habr Gedir activity.

- **Weather: High clouds, hot, good visibility.**
- **Terrain: Hills, flatlands, dry, some high grass.**
- **Enemy: None present, militia activity in neighboring villages.**
- **Friendly: Four Observation Posts (OPs) around village.**

2. Mission

- **Who: 10th Mtn. Platoon 3—Victor Three.**
- **What: Provide security during food distribution.**
- **When: Deploy when UNOSOM forces are ready.**

3. Execution

- **Commandor's Intent:** Prevent any disturbances that may interrupt food delivery, prevent civilian casualties.
- **Concept of Operation:** Platoon 3 will deploy by boat along with UNOSOM personnel to the food distribution point, where they will secure the perimeter and maintain order.
- **Coordinating Instructions:** Command will coordinate with UNOSOM commander.

4. Service and Support

- **Basic Load: M16, Beretta, Satchel Charge, Night-Vision Goggles.**

Summary of Mission

UN forces are attempting to distribute food and provisions to local civilians. Intel (intelligence) reports that prior attempts have been raided by militia intent on taking supplies for their clan's use. Prevent any militia unit from taking food shipments. Secure the village and ensure that enemy reinforcements cannot reach the UN convoy.

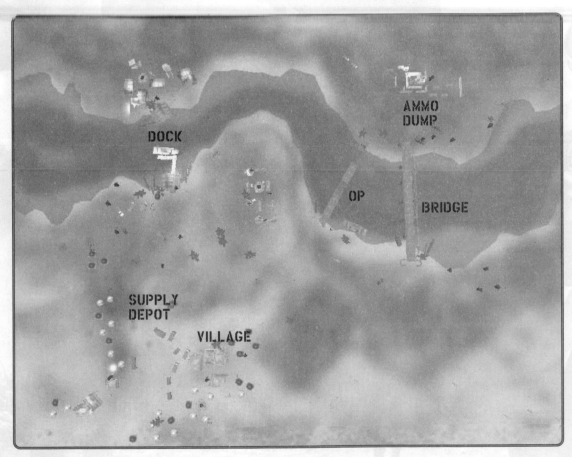

Village

PRIMA'S OFFICIAL STRATEGY GUIDE

Suggested Loadout

Primary Weapon: M16

Secondary Weapon: Beretta

Accessory: Satchel Charge

TIP *Take an M16-203 for your primary weapon. The grenade launcher gives you extra firepower for clearing out militia in the food-distribution area and clearing the bridge.*

TACTICS

1. Proceed to food drop-off point after the boat docks.

Your team arrives on the scene by boat.

Head for the food distribution area.

While the rest of your platoon is deploying with the food shipment, your team begins on the river. Move to the bow of the boat to join the rest of your team, then wait for the boat to dock. Check your weapons; you will have a fight on your hands when you reach shore. When the boat stops, hop onto the dock and follow your waypoint to the food distribution area.

2. Defend village from attacking militia.

TIP *Watch out for civilians. They are running out of the village when the shooting starts. Do not shoot civilians by mistake, thinking they are militia.*

Take cover behind some crates and clear out the area.

You will receive a new objective when you hear shots. Some militia have arrived and are trying to drive away the civilians so they can take the shipment. Move toward the village. Take cover behind some crates as you take out militia. A frag grenade or two does wonders on bunched-up enemies. Shoot until you clear out a group, then move forward to engage more.

Some flatbed trucks with militia arrive.

Take out the trucks before they can unload the militia.

By the time you clear out the first set of militia, more arrive. A couple flatbed trucks arrive. Take out the first truck before it stops and unloads the militia it carries. This is easier than having to individually eliminate each enemy. Clear out the second truck after it stops. Move along, following your waypoints and clearing the village as you go. There are other soldiers from your platoon who will help you in the village.

Move through the village so you can engage the enemy to the east.

Shoot at the technical until it bursts into flames.

After the village is clear, you receive a message that militia are approaching from the east. Reload your weapon, then head through the huts so you can cover the eastern approach. Use crates, vehicles, and buildings for cover and take out enemies as you see them. A technical will approach, so fire several bursts at it to deal with it. Continue firing until you receive word that the area is clear.

3. Proceed to the OP at the riverbank.

Now you must head to the riverbank to get some information from the soldiers stationed there. Follow your waypoints to a boat on the river. You can board the boat by walking across on the plank. In the boat you will find some ammo and a first aid kit. The soldiers there inform you that enemies on the other side of the river are crossing at the bridge. You must prevent this.

Meet up with the OP at the riverbank.

4. Take cover in the boat and suppress enemies from crossing the bridge.

Turn toward the bridge and press B to bring up your binoculars. If you look at the south end of the bridge, you will see a militia member behind some sandbags. Switch to your rifle and take him out. That clears the south end. However, more militia are trying to cross from the north. Stay near the OP, crouch down, and pick off enemies as they try to cross the bridge. A technical appears. A soldier from the OP will take out the technical by using his grenade launcher before the vehicle gets halfway across the bridge. Don't move. Another technical is on the way. Wait for the grenadier soldier to blow it up, then get ready to move.

Clear off anybody who tries to cross the bridge from the other side.

5. Cross the bridge and destroy the ammo cache on the far side.

TIP *The wrecked jeep at the north end of the bridge, on the western side, has a .50-caliber machinegun mounted on it. Though the jeep is not going anywhere, use the machinegun to help clear the area.*

Scan the ruins across the river for snipers.

Destroy the ammo crates with a satchel charge.

It is now time to cross the bridge. Move toward the south end. Use the binoculars to check the far side, then rush toward the burning wreckage on the bridge. Take cover behind it when you reach it. A couple of snipers are in the ruins north of the bridge. Use the binoculars to spot them, then drop them with a few bursts from your rifle. Once the area is clear, rush into the ruined building and plant a satchel charge near the crates of weapons. Then run back toward the bridge before using the detonator to blow the weapons sky high. Once you destroy them, you will have completed another of your objectives.

6. Fall back and plant a satchel charge on the bridge.

Place the demo charge in the middle of the bridge.

After you destroy the ammo dump, or sometime before, you get a message that enemy technicals are headed your way. Because you do not have the firepower to deal with them, it is time to get back to the other side of the river and prevent the enemy from crossing. Luckily, you have one demo charge left. Rush to the bridge and start moving across to the southern side. When you get to the middle of the bridge, press 7 to select the demo charge, then place it on the roadway of the bridge. Now hot-foot it to the end of the bridge.

7. Detonate charges from safe distance.

When your team is clear, blow the bridge.

Once you make it to the opposite river bank, follow the waypoints to the OP at the boat. Press 8 to select the detonator. Make sure your team is with you and safe, then use the detonator to set off the demo charge and bring the bridge's center span crashing into the river. After you accomplish this, the mission is complete.

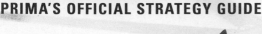

RIVER RAID

BRIEFING

OPORD: 0-93, 10th Mtn. Div. 0

Date Time: 270700 April 93

1. Situation

An informant has identified a village where a large weapons shipment is awaiting transfer to the Habr Gedir.

- **Weather: Dry and hot.**
- **Terrain: Village, few permanent structures, marshlands, and river nearby; UN marked minefield southeast of village.**
- **Enemy: Minimum of 20 Habr Gedir militia equipped with small arms patrolling village; technicals with .50-caliber mounted weapons.**
- **Friendly: None.**

2. Mission

- **Who: 10th Mtn. Platoon 3—Victor Three, Victor Two on standby.**
- **What: Insert by Black Hawk, locate and secure arms shipment.**
- **When: NLT (No Later Than) 1030 hours.**

3. Execution

- **Commander's Intent: Get in and out quickly. Secure arms shipment with no civilian casualties. Secondary objective is to gather intel and report to command.**
- **Concept of Operation: Move by vehicle along route Alpha to drop-off. Locate warehouse. Do actions on objective: Secure arms shipment and gather intel. Return by foot to extract vehicles and RTB (Return To Base).**
- **Coordinating Instructions: First Squad, assault and secure weapons. Second Squad on standby in Black Hawk.**

4. Service and Support

- **Basic Load: M16-203, Beretta, AT4.**

Summary of Mission

An informant has given us the location of an illegal weapons shipment waiting to be transferred to the Habr Gedir. Your team will be inserted by Black Hawk to the target area. Find and secure the weapons cache and retrieve any intel. Victor Two will be on standby if you need assistance.

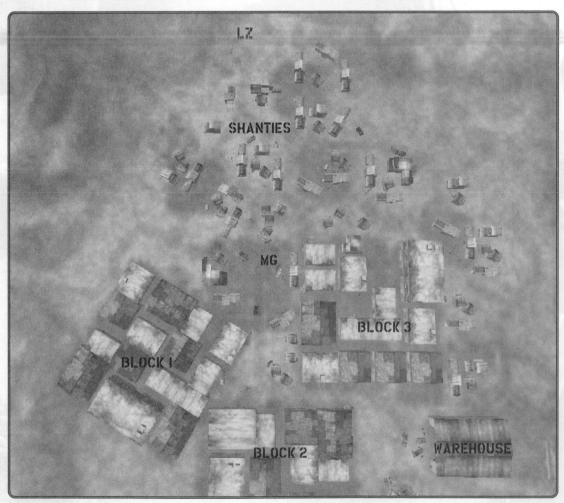

Village of Brava

Suggested Loadout

Primary Weapon: M16-203

Secondary Weapon: Beretta

Accessory: AT4

TACTICS

1. Proceed to town of Brava at waypoint Alpha.

Black Hawk will carry your team to Brava.

TIP *While moving through the village, be careful not to hit civilians. They move about and will run away and cower in a corner. However, at long range it's difficult to tell if a target is an enemy. Therefore, fire only at close range or into areas where you know there are no civilians.*

Your team begins aboard a Black Hawk flying toward the village of Brava. Don't worry about manning a minigun for the ride. You will not face any threats while airborne. Instead, prepare for fighting when you hit the ground. The chopper drops your team to the north of the village. As soon as you move south into the village, expect to take some fire from militia.

Rush for the village and the cover of the shanties.

Engage the militia at close range while you keep behind cover.

Instead of engaging at long range, from which you might accidentally hit civilians, run toward the edge of the shanties and use them for cover. Peek around corners to see if it is clear before running to the next shanty. Take out the militia as they come into your sights. The key is to attack while you are crouched and behind cover. If they shoot while you are out in the open, run for cover and drop into a crouch before returning fire.

Clear out the area around the wrecked technical.

Use the machinegun if necessary. It is great for dealing with a technical that drives around the area.

Move toward the machinegun mounted on a wrecked jeep. Keep your rifle set on semiautomatic fire. However, if a technical appears, switch to three-round burst mode to take it out quickly. As you move through the shanties, watch for enemies coming at you from your flanks. Most of them will approach from the south or east, so keep your guard up in those directions. Once you get to the machinegun, clear it of enemies. You can even take control of it to help clear the area around it in the middle of the village. However, don't stay long; you must reach the objective for the mission.

2. Secure arms warehouse by eliminating enemies there.

Move down the alleys of blocks 1 and 2 to avoid confronting the militia.

The arms shipment is located in the warehouse at the southeast corner of the village. Although your waypoints show a direct route to the objective, take the long way to the warehouse. From the machinegun, head for block 1 as shown on map for Brava. By moving through this area and on to block 2, you keep the enemies off to your left and approach the warehouse from the southwest. You could move through block 3, but you face enemies from the north, east, and south, because they expect you to come from that direction. Instead, by circling around the western and southern sides of the village, you will face less opposition.

Attack the warehouse.

Flank around to the right of the warehouse.

As you near the warehouse, make sure you have a full magazine loaded in your M16. Crouch and fire around a corner of a building toward the open doors of the warehouse. Be ready for lots of militia and a technical. Once you clear some of the enemies, rush to the small group of shanties southwest of the warehouse. Use the cover here to advance on the warehouse while engaging the militia as you move. Your team will follow you and provide fire support.

TIP *If the assault on the warehouse gets hot, toss a smoke grenade or two for concealment as you run across open areas.*

Clear out the militia hiding inside the warehouse.

By this time, your team heads into the warehouse. Keep up with them or lead the way. The interior is dark, making it difficult to locate enemies inside. Activate your night-vision goggles so you can see hiding militia inside. As you enter the warehouse, clear out the large open area, then go up the stairs on the right (south) side of the building. Follow the catwalk toward the rear of the building. Along the way, you see an open door below and to your right. Some militia are inside, so open fire, or lob a frag grenade inside to clear them out.

3. Search warehouse for arms shipment documents.

The intel is in the office at the back of the warehouse.

Once you have cleared the warehouse, you will be ordered to search for an intel. Move along the catwalk to the office at the rear of the warehouse, where you find some books. Pick them up; they provide information on another arms shipment. It seems that you will find more of the militia's arms in the village of Deka.

4. Get on the truck behind the warehouse and move out.

Hop into the back of the informant's truck.

Half of your team guards the warehouse, while you and another teammate head for Deka. Exit the door at the back of the warehouse to find a truck waiting to the east. Climb into the back of the truck, and the informant says he will take you to Deka. Once your teammate is aboard, the truck starts rolling.

Watch out for technicals along the road.

Don't expect a leisurely drive. Load your M16 and set it for three-round burst fire. As you drive, off to the right side of the road you will pass a wrecked technical with a working machinegun and a fully functional technical that chases after you. Destroy both, then get ready for another technical up ahead to the left. You cannot let them destroy your truck, kill the informant, or kill your teammate.

5. Rendezvous with support team, Victor Two, outside village of Deka.

TIP *Quick-save the game before entering the minefield. Crossing the minefield is tough at first, and you don't want to have to restart the mission if you take one wrong step.*

Step carefully through the minefield.

After getting past the technicals, the truck comes to a stop. Your informant tells you that there is a minefield up ahead, so you will have to continue on foot. Luckily, UN personnel have marked the mines for you. It is easiest to get through the minefield if you crouch down. This keeps your movement slow and controlled. The red stakes show mine locations, while the white stakes show a safe path through the minefield. Don't move around the outside of the minefield, or you will hit unmarked mines. Instead, move through the middle. Just look for lanes created by the white stakes that keep you as far away from red stakes as possible. Also, make sure your teammate is behind you before you enter the minefield. You don't want to get started and then have him come running to catch you—stepping on a mine along the way.

Watch out for the crocodiles.

Eventually, you make it out of the minefield. Move toward the river. Large crocodiles are just waiting to bite off your leg. Shoot these large reptiles as soon as you see them; don't let them get close to you or your teammate. Once you have cleared them out, cross the river as quickly as you can. Be ready for crocs on the opposite bank as well.

With your feet dry again, follow the waypoints to Victor Two. They are waiting for you along the road west of Deka. By now you are probably running low on ammo and may have taken some hits along the way. Not to worry. There is a first-aid kit and some ammo where Victor Two is positioned.

6. Proceed to Deka.

7. Secure Deka at waypoint Hotel by eliminating the enemies there.

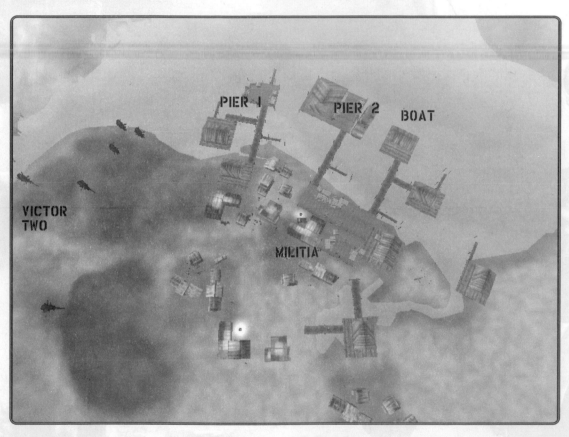

Village of Deka

Militia wait to ambush you at the crossroads.

Having met up with Victor Two, it is time to head into Deka. Your teams head east along the road right toward the village. Just outside of the village, you run into some militia at a crossroad. Take them out and keep moving. Approach the village by moving to the north of the road. A large concentration of militia are located in the middle of Deka. However, while you need to engage some of the enemy, you must also secure the arms on one of the docks.

Go to Pier 1 as shown on the Deka map. As you move along the riverbank, you face militia mostly to your front and right. Stop to take a few shots, clear your way, and then keep moving. The arms you seek are on Pier 2.

You have to be careful of civilians in Deka, so watch your shots.

8. Destroy the weapons transport boat before it escapes.

Use the AT4 to sink the arms boat.

As you approach Pier 2, you receive new orders. It seems that the weapons have been loaded onto a boat, which is about to escape from Deka. If you can catch sight of the pier before the boat leaves, shoot at the barrels of gasoline on the dock next to the boat. When they explode, they might destroy the boat as well. However, if that does not work, run as fast as you can to the pier. Aim the AT4 at the fleeing boat and fire. One shot will send the boat to the bottom of the river and prevent the Habr Gedir from receiving the shipment of arms. Once the boat is destroyed, the mission is complete.

TIP *While running out onto Pier 2 to engage the boat, you can be a little less cautious than usual. Even if you take some hits, once the boat is history, the mission is over. However, watch out for enemy fire from behind and from the boat. If they hit the gasoline barrels while you are nearby, you may be toasted.*

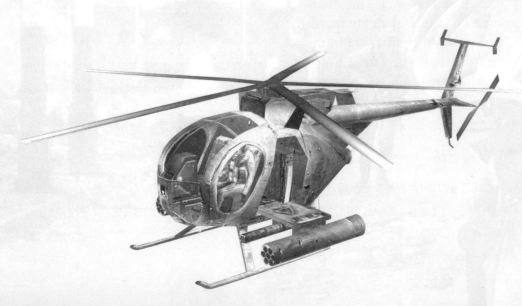

GASOLINE ALLEY

BRIEFING

OPORD: 1-93, TFR

Date Time: 272015 August 93

1. Situation

Aidid's financial chief, Osman Otto, operates a warehouse in Mogadishu where they are outfitting pickup trucks with .50-caliber machineguns that threaten UNOSOM II forces.

- **Weather: High clouds, low light.**
- **Terrain: Urban.**
- **Enemy: Intel places guards at the perimeters and along your ingress, but no fortified positions. Strong Habr Gedir presence, possibility of reinforcements from neighboring area. Guard and protect possible access routes.**

2. Mission

- **Who: Ranger Platoons 2 and 3.**
- **What: Insert by Humvee, locate and destroy technicals.**
- **When: 2015 hours (dusk) depart Task Force Ranger base at Mogadishu airport.**

3. Execution

- **Commander's Intent: Secure and destroy technicals. All forces return to base.**
- **Two teams of Rangers will infiltrate and make the final assault on foot along route Red. Teams will get as deep as possible into enemy territory before enemy can raise an alarm.**
- **Coordinating Instructions: Platoon 4 will extract all personnel once action on the objective is complete.**

4. Service and Support

- **Basic Load: Night-Vision Goggles, M16, M9 Beretta, Satchel Charges.**

Summary of Mission

We have our first mission for Task Force Ranger today. We need to capture the technicals being outfitted with machineguns and destroy them.

Suggested Loadout

Primary Weapon: CAR-15

Secondary Weapon: Beretta

Accessory: Satchel charge

TIP *The default primary weapon for this mission is the M16. However, for this type of operation, the automatic-fire mode of the CAR-15 come in handy.*

TACTICS

1. Protect the convoy from enemy fire.

You are riding into enemy territory.

You begin the mission aboard a Humvee, taking control of a mounted machinegun. For this first phase, your Humvee drives alongside a convoy of trucks and other Humvees providing an escort for them. You have an unlimited amount of ammunition, so feel free to use all you need.

Use the binoculars to locate enemies ahead.

Mow down enemies in the alleys as you drive past.

Groups of militia run out into the road to attack the convoy.

Once the convoy gets rolling, start looking around. Use the binoculars to look down the street, keeping a watch along the roofline for enemies waiting to ambush you. Because it is dusk, the night-vision goggles a great help in locating enemies, which can be difficult to see. In addition to militia on the roofs, enemies hiding down alleys that run perpendicular to the road, in small courtyard areas, and even directly in front of the convoy in the roadway will engage you. Although some civilians are at the beginning of the convoy's drive, once you get into the thick of the fight, almost all those on foot around the convoy are enemies. Keep the machinegun rockin' and rollin' as you clear the way for the convoy. A Little Bird provides air support toward the end of this run.

2. Advance on the garage, neutralize any resistance.

When the convoy halts at the perimeter, hop off and get ready to move out on foot.

Use the shacks for cover as you engage militia on the shipping containers.

Eventually, your convoy comes to a halt. You must lead your team the rest of the way to the garage on foot. Dismount the Humvee, set your rifle to semiautomatic mode, and get ready to go. Follow your waypoints toward the garage. If you get lost, follow your teammates. You encounter enemy fire from several directions. However, unless the fire comes from your forward area as you advance, continue moving until you reach cover—then you can crouch and return fire. If the enemy is in front of you, engage as you advance.

Expect militia to shoot at you from your front, the sides, and especially from above. They like to stand on large shipping containers as they try to kill you and your team. Some are difficult to see, so use your binoculars to find them, then the scoped view of your primary weapon to line up the sights and take them out.

The garage is just up ahead on the left.

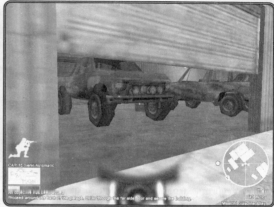

Crouch so you can enter the garage.

Although you can take your time and try to clear the way to the garage, it is usually best to just keep moving and only engage enemies in your path. Use the shanties for cover as you head toward the first waypoint. Take cover next to a bombed out building. Take out the two snipers on the roof directly ahead of you. Then quickly turn the corner and shoot the two militiamen on the second floor. Aim at the front of the garage that your teammates are attacking and help them wipe out the militia on the ground and on the roof. Move to the corner of the warehouse on your left. Peek around the corner and deal with the militia surrounding the fire barrel. As you move through grid D,4 to D,5, use the large shipping containers as cover on your flanks along with buildings. With your right and left sides protected by these structures, concentrate your attention, and fire, on what is in front of you. When you reach grid C,5, you must cross an open area. However, the garage is right in front of you. Instead of getting into duels with snipers on the rooftops while you are exposed, run for the doors to the garage. They are only partially opened, so you must quickly crouch to duck inside.

3. Clear the garage interior of militia.

When you first enter the garage, you are in an area with three technicals lined up. These must be destroyed before you leave, but forget about it for now. Instead, concentrate on clearing out the entire garage. Follow the waypoints east into a large area in the center of the garage building. Take out the militia straight ahead through the doorway. More are to the right of this large room and in another room to the left.

Clear out the militia directly ahead in the large area.

Pull out a frag grenade and throw it into the room on your left as you face the large area. Pull out a flashbang and throw it into the middle of the large area where they are working on trucks. Switch back to your rifle, wait for the flashbang to explode, then rush into the large area and clear it. Concentrate on the militia on the ground floor and the one up on the catwalk. Head into the small room where you threw the frag grenade. Grab the first-aid kit in this room. You can also get more ammo from the armory in this room.

Two militia are in the room to the left.

4. Defend your position until convoy arrives.

A technical bursts into the garage.

Shoot at the tangos as they try to enter the garage.

Once the garage area is clear, an enemy technical crashes through the large doors of the garage and into the open area below you. Destroy the technical, then be ready for waves of militia to come pouring in through the breach. Grenades work well, as does automatic fire. Try to take them out at the doorway before they can enter the garage. Watch your ammo and reload during the brief lulls. Toss grenades at the groups that gather at the right and left openings to the garage. You can also try "running and gunning" or the opposite, lying prone and shooting the enemies.

5. Plant satchel charges on technicals in garage.

Drop a satchel charge by the technicals.

After you have repelled the militia assaulting the garage, you receive word that the convoy is approaching. It is time to make your getaway. Go downstairs to the ground level. Remember those three technicals parked in the garage on the western side? Drop a satchel charge on one of them.

6. Board the trucks and detonate your satchels.

With the charge planted, exit the garage through the breach in the large area. Don't worry about blowing the charges with the detonator. When you reach the convoy and the mission ends, they detonate, taking those technicals with them.

Head for the convoy to complete the mission.

BESIEGED

BRIEFING

UPORD: 4-93, TFR Div. 3

Date Time: 051300 May 93

1. Situation

A convoy of Pakistani UN soldiers is under heavy fire in grid Charlie Two. They have at least one truck destroyed and are surrounded.

- **Weather: Hot, sunny.**
- **Terrain: City, urban.**
- **Enemy: Minimum of 40 Habr Gedir militia, AK 47s, possible RPGs, and Technicals.**
- **Friendly: None.**

2. Mission

- **Who: Ranger Team Two-One.**
- **What: Insert by Humvee. Locate, reinforce, and free the trapped convoy.**
- **When: Immediately following briefing.**

3. Execution

- **Commander's Intent: Quickly locate Pakistanis, reinforce their position, and facilitate their escape.**
- **Concept of Operation: Move by vehicle to UN forces, set up a secure perimeter, and work to dismantle any resistance and roadblocks that prevent their movement.**
- **Coordinating Instructions: 1st Squad assault.**

4. Service and Support

- **Basic Load: CAR-15-203, Beretta, Satchel Charge.**

Summary of Mission

Get your team to the trapped Pakistanis quickly. Secure their position, then help them get past the roadblock.

Suggested Loadout

Primary Weapon: M16

Secondary Weapon: Beretta

Accessory: Satchel charge

TIP *Your default loadout is an M16. However, for this mission, the automatic fire of the CAR-15 is a great help, as is the attached grenade launcher, which does a good job of clearing out enemy snipers.*

TACTICS

1. Make your way to the ambushed Pakistani convoy.

You begin in a Humvee on your way to the rescue.

You begin the mission behind a .50-caliber machinegun mounted on a Humvee. During the first bit, hold your fire. Only innocent civilians are running around. However, after the second or third turn, your rescue convoy starts taking fire. Use your binoculars to look ahead for trouble, but be careful not to get tunnel vision. You will face several threats from your flanks.

Watch for enemies near the merchant carts.

Your first real enemies appear near waypoint Bravo. Fire away at the merchant carts to take out the militia hiding behind them. Be especially alert for warnings of RPGs ahead or to your sides. As soon as you discover an RPG, it should be your main target. Take out the militia soldier firing one of these weapons quickly, because a direct hit destroys your Humvee—killing you and ending the mission.

After passing through waypoint Charlie and heading on to Delta, be ready for some enemy technicals. They drive across the road or drive along in front of you firing a heavy machinegun at your convoy. Pour on the lead and destroy these vehicles before they cause you damage.

The technicals move fast and are hard to hit unless you engage them as soon as they come into sight.

You can expect a couple of soldiers with RPGs near the market area. Be ready to shoot them down as soon as they appear.

Waypoint Echo is located in a market area that your Humvee will drive around. Hopefully you will have destroyed the technicals before you reach this point. However, if they got away from you, here is where they will wait. Shoot at anything that moves. Because you do not need to worry about ammo, don't stop firing.

Once you reach waypoint Foxtrot, your rescue convoy halts. Lead your team the rest of the way on foot. Dismount and move to the buildings on the right (to the east of the Humvees). Watch out for militia coming down the streets toward you (from both the north and south), as well as shooting down at you from the upstairs windows overlooking the street.

You must go the rest of the way on foot.

2. Eliminate snipers attacking the rear of the convoy.

Shortly after dismounting, you receive a new objective. You now must clear the streets and buildings near the rear of the stalled Pakistani convoy. The key to this part of the mission is patience and firepower. If you run for it, you will take fire from several directions at once. Plus, you would have to go back and clear out the buildings later anyway. Therefore, advance methodically down the street, clearing as you go.

Watch for militia up in the second and third floors of buildings along the road.

Stay close to a wall on your right as you move down the street. Use vehicles and other objects as cover. Although it's tedious, move a little bit and then stop to engage any enemies you can see. The militia in the upstairs windows are difficult to see when they hide in the shadows. Therefore, as a general rule, fire a burst into each window or opening just to make sure it is clear.

Keep your team close by and don't let them get killed. If it becomes too hot, order them to stay put, then call them into action as needed.

A first-aid kit and some ammo—these are a few of my favorite things.

Keep advancing down the street until you reach waypoint Kilo. A small alley is south of this waypoint. There is a first-aid kit and some ammo near a wounded Pakistani soldier. Grab them, because you will probably need both. By the time you reach Kilo, you should receive a new objective. If not, it means that you may have missed some militia near the rear of the convoy. Backtrack and hunt them down. Because you were hugging the walls on one side of the street, look up into the windows on that side as you return. Often this is where you can find an enemy or two who you bypassed during your advance.

3. Take out those enemies in the bombed out building at waypoint Hotel and the snipers across the street.

Once you have achieved your second objective, you receive your third. Continue past Kilo and on to waypoint Lima. As you approach the front of the convoy, you take fire from the west, which is to your left. Again, move slowly and clear your way in.

Use the trucks as cover from the sniper fire above.

When you arrive at waypoint Lima, clear the outside area to the west, then activate your night-vision goggles and head into the building to the east. Often an enemy is just to the south after you enter. Drop him, then turn north and head for the hallway. Before you rush down the hallway, wait a second and pick off any militia that run out. Now move into the hall.

Drop anybody that moves through the hallway.

There is a main room off to the left that you can see, and shoot into, through the rubble of a wall. There are also a couple of rooms to the right. Clear these as you watch for militia in the main room. Use your frag grenades to clear a room before you enter. Once you have cleared the main room, head upstairs to the second floor.

TIP *If you need it, a first-aid kit is in the western part of the first floor of the bombed-out building.*

As usual, advance with caution. Several enemies are on the second floor. When you get to the landing halfway up, throw a frag grenade up the stairs and to the right. As soon as it detonates, aim toward the right and move up the rest of the way to the second floor. Be ready for enemies ahead, left, and right when you reach the top. Just mow them down as you find some cover. Take a breather and reload if necessary, then clear out the second floor. As you do, go to the southeast corner of the floor and locate stairs to the rooftop.

Head up the stairs and fire at any targets that come into sight.

Be ready to clear out snipers on the rooftop.

Crouch and slowly move up the stairs. A few militia are on the roof—if you did not eliminate them when you were down on the street. Clear all enemies on the roof, then take out snipers in the windows across the street to the west. Head to the western edge of the roof and fire into the street at any other militia. Follow the edge to the north, then around to the east, clearing the streets as you go.

4. Destroy roadblock at waypoint Juliet.

Fire down into the streets.

Throw a grenade around this corner.

Finish off this militia ambush before you head to the roadblock.

Once you have neutralized all the militia, you receive a new objective. However, don't rush down to accomplish it right away. The enemy has an ambush in store if you are not careful. Return to the first floor. Instead of going out into the street to the west, exit the building through one of the holes in the eastern walls. This puts you out in an alley. Follow it north. When you come to an intersection, halt and pull out a frag grenade. Throw it around the corner to the right. Wait for it to detonate, then move around the corner to engage an enemy at an emplaced machinegun. Although the grenade does the job, be ready to shoot if necessary.

Throw a satchel charge on the roadblock.

Blow the roadblock to complete the mission.

By this time, you should have eliminated all enemies in the area. All that remains is to remove the roadblock. Continue to waypoint November. When you arrive, pull out a satchel charge and place it on the roadblock. Head south down the street to avoid being caught in the blast. When ready, use the detonator to set off the charge and clear the road for the Pakistani convoy to continue on its way. Mission accomplished.

RADIO AIDID

BRIEFING

OPORD: 3-93, TFR

Date Time: 030200 September 93

1. Situation

The Habr Gedir clan is operating a radio station in Mogadishu that is broadcasting anti-UN propaganda throughout the region.

- **Weather: Dark, moonless night.**
- **Terrain: City center, urban.**
- **Enemy: Outlying guard posts, minimum 15 militia inside radio station.**
- **Friendly: None**

2. Mission

- **Who: Delta Teams 5 and 2, Ranger 4-2 (Transports).**
- **What: Stealth insertion, destroy radio transmitter, control room, and generators.**
- **When: 0200 hours.**

3. Execution

- **Commander's Intent: Eliminate Aidid's transmitting capabilities.**
- **Concept of Operation: Delta Team 5 will make a stealth insertion without raising alarms and secure the radio building using room-takedown techniques. Use silenced MP5's to eliminate guards if needed. Once in control, satchel charges are to be set. Extract after actions on objective.**
- **Coordinating Instructions: Delta 5-1 will lead the assault on the building. Ranger 4-2 will maintain distance and vehicle security until extraction.**

4. Service and Support

- **Basic Load: Night-Vision Goggles, MP5, Colt .45, Satchel Charges.**

Summary of Mission

You have been ordered to undertake a stealth raid after nightfall to take the Habr Gedir radio station in Mogadishu off the air.

Suggested Loadout

Primary Weapon: MP5

Secondary Weapon: Colt .45

Accessory: Satchel charges

TACTICS

1. Proceed to the radio building at waypoint Radio Building.

This mission requires your team to maintain stealth as much as possible. In some of the previous missions, you may have found that the night-vision goggles are useful for seeing enemies in shadows or during night missions. However, for this mission during a new moon, the night-vision goggles are absolutely essential. Without them, you will not be able to see anything in the dark.

Activate your night-vision goggles and get ready to move out.

Advance quietly through the alleys and roads to avoid detection.

Use the binoculars to check the area ahead for militia. Most of them are near the fire barrels.

The first phase of the mission is not difficult. Lead your team to the radio building. The streets are pitch-black except for a few fire barrels. The waypoints take you on a roundabout path to your objective. You will be moving down narrow alleys, along roads, and even through some open areas. Hug the walls and don't walk out in the open. You will come across militia along the way, both individually and in pairs. Around the fire cans you can expect larger groups of four to six. Although you will have to take out the small patrols, leave the concentrations alone. A firefight will alert the rest.

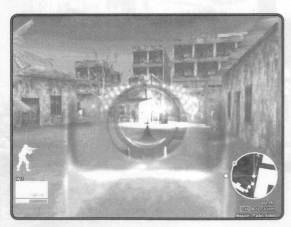

You will have to take out some small groups that block your way to the target building.

A good tactic for moving to the target building as safely as possible is to take your time. Move through narrow alleys that cover your flanks. Before going around a corner, prepare to take down any enemy who might be on the other side. After ensuring that the immediate area is clear, take out the binoculars and scan for more militia ahead. Because it is so dark, distant enemies will not be able to see you unless you move through an area lit by a light source such as a fire barrel. By advancing with caution, you should make it to the radio building without any major firefights, simply by following the waypoints.

2. Secure the bottom floor and destroy the power generator at waypoint Generator.

The entrance to the building is fairly nondescript.

After stunning the militia inside with a flashbang, clear out the first floor.

Blow up this generator with a satchel charge.

When you arrive at the radio building, enter through a door on the ground floor, but before rushing in, throw a flashbang into the room and initiate a room takedown. After stunning the militia in the main room, enter and take them down. There are two other rooms, one to the north and another to the west, that contain several militia. Use a flashbang in each before entering and clearing. Be aware that 4–5 militia will come charging out of the room at the end of the hall. After you have cleared the entire first floor, move into the room with the generator and plant a satchel charge. Exit the room, then detonate the charge. Not only does this cut the power to the radio, but also to the lights in the building, thereby giving your team the advantage.

3. Destroy radio equipment on the top floor of radio building at waypoint Transmitter.

Head up the stairs to the top floor, taking out the militia along the way.

After destroying the generator, it is time to head for the stairs. The radio room is on the top floor, so you have to climb several flights. Expect a couple of militia at the landing of each floor. If you are having trouble, throw a flashbang or frag grenade ahead to stun or clear the way.

Order your team to clear the large room at the top.

Toss a flashbang in the radio room.

Use your satchel charge to take out the radio equipment.

When you reach the top floor, lead your team over to a doorway. If you need health at this point, head up the ladder to your left and retrieve the first aid. Then climb back down to continue your mission. When they are all assembled, press backspace to order them to enter and clear the room. One of your team throws in a flashbang before the entire team rushes in. Clear this main room before heading to the radio room. As before, throw a flashbang (or frag grenade if you are out of flashbangs) into the room before moving in. After you clear it, plant your second satchel charge near the radio equipment, leave the room, and detonate it. If for some reason the charge does not take out the equipment, use your submachine gun or pistol to do the job.

4. Destroy the radio tower at waypoint Tower.

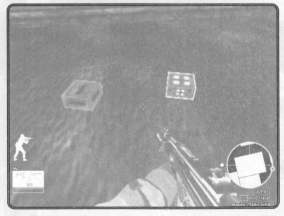

Pick up the ammo and the first aid kit on the roof.

Plant a satchel charge at the base of the tower.

There is one more objective for you to destroy. Head up the ladder in the radio room; it takes you to the roof. Move out toward the radio-transmission tower. You are all out of satchel charges by this time. Don't worry, near the tower is a first-aid kit (if you did not grab it earlier) and some ammo, which includes a couple more satchel charges. Place one at the base of the tower, then return to the ladder. Before descending back into the radio room, detonate the charge to complete another objective.

5. Get back to the Humvees near the insertion point at waypoint Extract.

Prepare for trouble the second you step outside the building.

With Aidid's radio station off the air, it is now time to get out. If you cleared the building as you advanced up to the radio room, you should meet no resistance on the way down. However, as you exit the building, expect some trouble. The explosions have attracted reinforcements—including a technical.

You must engage the militia right outside the building. When you have put down this force of resistance, get moving. Follow the waypoints on the GPS map along a route similar to the one you took to the radio building. A lot more militia are looking for your team, so be ready. Make sure your weapon is fully loaded before moving across an open area. A Black Hawk will orbit the area, mowing down militia with its miniguns. The best tactic is to keep moving. Fight only when you must clear an area to continue your advance. Keep an eye on the other operators in your team. Don't get so far ahead that they are left behind, making them easy targets for the enemy.

Make your way back through the city to the extraction point.

Shoot the gunners on the technicals.

Run for the Humvees of the convoy coming to pick you up.

The militia is waiting to ambush your team near waypoint Whiskey. They have two technicals blocking your path to the convoy. You do not have to destroy the technicals. Instead, take out the enemy manning the machinegun on each to eliminate them as a threat. Once both technicals are neutralized, run for the convoy at waypoint X-Ray to complete the mission.

RUSSIAN UNDERGROUND

BRIEFING

OPORD: 5-93, TFR

Date Time: 100700 September 93

1. Situation

A number of high-ranking Habr Gedir leaders and militia are planning a strategy meeting this afternoon in a former Soviet military complex.

- **Weather: Hazy, hot, high clouds.**
- **Terrain: City center, urban.**
- **Enemy: Unknown. At least 20 militia. Possible technicals.**
- **Friendly: None.**

2. Mission

- **Who: Delta Teams 1, 3, 5, 160th SOAR, Ranger 4-2 (Transports).**
- **What: Helo insert, secure Habr Gedir officials.**
- **When: 1545 hours.**

3. Execution

- **Commander's Intent: Capture as many Habr Gedir as possible while avoiding civilian casualties.**
- **Concept of Operation: All teams will make a fast insertion via helo into the center of the complex. Teams will split up, secure prisoners, and meet Platoon 4 at the extraction point.**

4. Service and Support

- **Basic Load: CAR-15, Colt .45, Satchel Charges.**

5. Command and Signal

Task Force chain of command in effect. Command will coordinate from base. Hand and arm signals tactical standard operating procedure (TACSOP), with higher via FM primary and satellite communications (SATCOM) alternate. Standard unit communication electronics operating instruction (CEOI).

Summary of Mission

We have reports of a large Habr eadir clan meeting happening today in a complex built by the Soviets. We're sending in teams to capture as many as we can find. If we're lucky, one will talk and give us information on Aidid.

Suggested Loadout

Primary Weapon: CAR-15

Secondary Weapon: Colt .45

Accessory: Satchel Charges

TACTICS

1. Secure the second floor to the Russian Embassy Compound.

Gather your team on the rooftop and locate one of the two skylights.

This is a pretty exciting mission with lots of action. Your team begins aboard a Black Hawk flying you to the target building. When it starts to set down on the roof of the Russian embassy, get ready to jump out onto the rooftop. There are no enemies on the roof, so get your team together and head over to one of two skylights. The Northern skylight will provide an easier entry as you will drop into an empty room.

After stunning the enemy below, drop down through the skylight.

Cover the hallway leading to the large room.

The skylights are your way down into the embassy. Pull out a flashbang and throw it through the skylight and down into the second floor. When it detonates, jump up onto the skylight and drop into the room. Clear out the room, then take up a position to cover the hallway leading toward the main room on this floor. Wait for the rest of your team to join you on the second floor, then begin clearing each of the small rooms branching off from the hallway.

Clear out the large main room. Watch for militia hiding in the corners.

With the small rooms cleared, continue to the main room and clear it. Continue down the other hallway, clearing out the side rooms and the larger room at the end. Once the entire second floor is clear, head back to the main room and locate the stairway. While waiting for your team to reassemble, cover the stairway and take out any enemies who climb up.

2. Rendezvous with team 2 on the first floor.

When the second floor is reported clear, lead your team down the stairway to the first floor. Watch your fire when you get down to this floor. Team 2 should have already cleared it out and you don't want to hit any teammates. Advance along the waypoints to meet up with the Team 2 leader, and you will receive new orders.

Team 2 is on the floor directly below where you entered the building.

3. Go to the basement and breach the bunker door.

It seems the other teams are stuck in the basement. The tier-one officials have entered a bunker complex under the embassy. They need you to breach the bunker door.

Lead your team down into the basement. Again, watch your fire; only friendlies are here. Advance to the end of the basement and a large door. Plant a satchel charge next to the door, then move back. Detonate the charge to blow in the bunker door and allow the teams to continue their pursuit.

Plant a satchel charge by the door.

4. Find a way down one floor and secure it.

The tier-one officials are escaping. You cannot shoot through the bulletproof window.

Here is the trap door.

Once the door is gone, you will see enemies moving behind a large window. You cannot shoot them as the window is reinforced and bulletproof. However, not all of the militia have escaped. Head into the rooms to the left and clear them out. Look for a trapdoor leading down to a level below. After the rooms are clear, look in the northwest corner to find the trapdoor.

Clear out the entire lower level. It is crawling with militia.

Drop through the hole in the floor. There are a number of militia on this level. Throw a flashbang over to the south to stun them, then rush in to take them down before they can react. Be especially cautious of militia hiding behind boxes or furniture. You may think an area is clear, only to be shot in the back as you continue through the room. After all enemies on this level have been neutralized, head to the stairway in the northeastern part of the room and head down to a lower level. If you received a message that the area is clear, then chances are that no one will be down here. However, if you have not been given such a message, be ready for more trouble. Even if the level is clear, it is a good idea to head downstairs. A first-aid kit and some ammo are there. This room can also be accessed by another trapdoor in the northeast corner.

5. Go upstairs to the room where the Tier One officials were.

Follow the tier-one officials into this tunnel.

With the lower level clear, it is time to return upstairs. At the stairway, take the stairs up to the room on the other side of the large window. The enemies are nowhere to be found. However, there is an entrance to some tunnels. This is the only way the tier-one officials could have gone.

6. Pursue the Tier One officials into the tunnels.

Continue your pursuit of the tier-one officials into the tunnel. You definitely need night-vision goggles in certain parts of the tunnels. Using them throughout may result in missing some key items. There are no branches in the tunnel, so don't worry about getting lost. However, be wary about the militia waiting to ambush you around many of the corners in the tunnel or hiding in alcoves off the sides. Although the mission seems to be pushing you to rush and get through the tunnels quickly, you can and should take your time. Keep your rifle set on automatic so you can easily fire a burst to mow down enemies before they can get the drop on you. Use the "lean" feature to look around corners and take out unsuspecting milita.

Watch out for militia everywhere in the tunnels.

An enemy mans a machinegun.

Militiamen run for the machinegun as soon as you take out one gunner.

Pick up the ammo and first-aid kit.

As you move through the tunnels, you run into militia—until you approach waypoint Quebec. Off to the south of Quebec is a room with a machinegun. Several militiamen wait here to mow down your entire team. Therefore, as you approach this waypoint, be ready. Throw a frag grenade around a corner to try and take out the machinegun, which is shown on your GPS map. If that does not work, try a flashbang and rush in. Clear this entire room of enemies. Pick up the first-aid kit and ammo. Continue down the tunnels to the end.

TIP *Don't feel safe because you shot the enemy manning the machinegun. If other enemies are in the area, they will quickly run to the machinegun and take up the role of gunner.*

![Delta Force Black Hawk Down - Prima's Official Strategy Guide]

7. Exit the tunnels and reach the Black Hawk for extraction.

Climb the ladder to exit the tunnels.

The tier-one officials are secured.

Head for the Black Hawk and a ride back to base.

Just before you reach the tunnel exit, there is an alcove containing a stack of boxes. Destroy these boxes to reveal first aid and ammo. The tunnel eventually dead-ends with a ladder leading up to the surface. Climb the ladder into a small building. By this time, the tier-one officials have already exited the building. Follow them out of the building and to the west. Follow the waypoints around and to the south.

CAUTION *Do not shoot the officials! If you kill them, the mission will end in a failure.*

Do not take out the officials. Instead, follow them to the extraction area. Along the way you must neutralize several militiamen. However, when you reach the large open area near where you will extract (grid F,6), be ready for some heavy resistance. Militia here, armed with RPGs, can not only ruin your day, but also shoot down the Black Hawks which are your ride home. Quickly deal with them, then locate the tier-one officials. They are in the southwestern corner of the fenced-in area. Another team has already secured them. Complete the mission by getting to the Black Hawk, which landed east of your location.

SHATTERED PALACE

BRIEFING

OPORD: 6-93, TFR

Date Time: 171045 September 93

1. Situation

There is a mansion at grid reference X-Ray One, where a number of Tier-One personalities will be meeting tonight. Aidid is expected to be in attendance.

- **Weather: Hazy, low light, hot.**
- **Terrain: City center, urban.**
- **Enemy: 30–40 militia with AK-47s, RPGs, and possible technicals.**
- **Friendly: None.**

2. Mission

- **Who: Delta Teams 4, 5, 160th SOAR , Ranger 4-2. (Transports)**
- **What: Helo insert, 5-1 provides security and 4-1 secures Habr Gedir officials.**
- **When: 1545 hours.**

3. Execution

- **Commander's Intent: Provide security for assault force, aid extraction of prisoners.**
- **Concept of Operation: Team Five-One will insert by Little Bird and cover Team Four's fast rope insert. Five-One will proceed to outlying building "A" and take it down to prevent reinforcements. Once clear, Five-One will clear the courtyard, regroup at the main target building, and provide security for extraction.**

4. Service and Support

- **Basic Load: CAR-15/M203, Shotgun, Claymores, Night-Vision Goggles.**

Summary of Mission

A number of tier-one personalities will meet tonight in an old hotel complex in the city. Aidid is expected to attend. Our teams will secure the complex and capture any Habr Gedir personnel. There will be many civilians in the area, so check your fire.

Suggested Loadout

Primary Weapon: CAR-15-203

Secondary Weapon: Shotgun

Accessory: Claymores

TACTICS

1. Protect Delta Team 4 while they infil building "B."

This can be a very tough mission. You will be shot at from every direction, so take it slow and easy. The key is to clear as you go, leaving no enemies behind that can sneak up and attack you from the rear.

Fly to your objective building in a Little Bird.

TIP *Although three first-aid kits are scattered about, there are no ammo boxes in this mission. The CAR-15 is set on full automatic by default, but this setting exhausts your ammo before you complete the mission. Change your rate of fire to semiautomatic and keep it there—you'll be lucky to have more than a magazine remaining at the end of the mission.*

This is another helo insertion. You begin the mission riding on the skid benches of a Little Bird. Keep an eye on the GPS map to see how close you are to your target building. The helo will stop to hover after a sharp banked turn and you will need to take out the RPG militia standing on the archway. Use your scope. After a short flight, the Little Bird goes into a second hover over a building Delta Team 4 is attempting to infiltrate. You must take out all of the militia gathered on the roof to ensure their (and your) success. The easiest way to do this is to use the grenade launcher. Aim at the 2 main groups of militia, and bombs away. Finish off the few survivors with semiautomatic rounds. Now you are ready to hit your target building. The Little Bird circles around the area before putting down on the roof.

2. Secure Building "A" at waypoint Echo by eliminating all enemies there.

TIP *The flashbang is your friend for this mission. You have five to start. Toss a flashbang in nearly every large room before you enter.*

Drop a flashbang through the trapdoor.

Clear the upper level.

Secure the rooftop, then locate the trapdoor leading down into the building. Unless you want to die as you drop down the ladder, hold up. Pull out a flashbang and drop it through the trapdoor. Quickly switch back to your rifle, activate your night-vision goggles, and wait for the grenade to detonate. As soon as it goes off, drop to the second level and neutralize the stunned militia. You should be able to take them out before they shoot.

However, only those on the second level are stunned. As soon as your team drops down, be ready for militia coming up the stairs from the ground level. In fact, as you move across the second level, clearing as you go, take up a position at the top of the stairs and drop anyone coming up.

Now take down the lower level of the building.

Once your team is in position next to you, press [backspace] to order them to clear the downstairs level. They throw a flashbang to the ground below, then rush down the stairs to eliminate the enemies before they can recover. Because most of the militia downstairs will be stunned, your main threat comes from the doorway leading out of the building. More militia fire through the doorway at your team.

Once the building is secure, use the first-aid kit in the back corner if necessary. This is also a good spot to do a quick save.

3. Clear and cross the courtyard to building "B" at waypoint Hotel.

With the first building clear, it is time to head to the main target building, where the other Delta Team has captured the militia leaders. Unfortunately, you must clear the large courtyard, which is crawling with enemies. Also, just outside the building at Bravo are two mounted machineguns and a parked technical. Those machineguns are a major threat and will chew up your team if not dealt with carefully.

Hold in the first building while clearing out the courtyard.

Before running out into the courtyard, use the current building as an initial fire position. Stay inside and shoot through the doorway at any enemies you see. Deactivate your night-vision goggles so you can see enemies at longer distances. There is one enemy outside the door and to the left, so take him out before getting too close to the doorway. From the building, you can clear out most of the courtyard south of your position. All that remains is the area to the west.

Crouch down and carefully exit the building. Keep the building on your right shoulder as you move west. This will keep your right flank secure—at least for the length of the building. Most threats come from the area around the fountain in the center of the courtyard. Stop and deal with each before continuing. When you reach the corner of the building, turn right (north), then strafe left around the corner. A couple of militia wait to ambush your force as they clear the corner. Drop them first.

It is now time to deal with those machinegun positions. They are shown on your GPS map, represented by an "E" surrounded by a circle. While crouched down, you won't see them, but they will fire at you. You can either use your binoculars to locate them, or line up your sights by using the GPS map. It is easiest to deal with all resistance around the fountain before taking on the emplacements. Take out the one on the left first with a grenade from your rifle-mounted M203 launcher. It may take a couple to eliminate this threat. For the second position, repeat the process. With the main threats in the courtyard dealt with, move out. Instead of moving through the fountain area, head to the north of it. Jump over the low wall and move to the entrance of the main target building. Dispatch any remaining militia on the way.

Use the grenade launcher to take out a machinegun position across the courtyard.

4. Secure building "B" at waypoint Hotel by eliminating all enemies there.

Clear out the lobby area of the second building before entering.

Watch for reinforcements to come from the back of the building.

The interior of the building at Bravo crawls with militia. Before entering, stay outside and shoot at enemies through the doorway. There are several enemies upstairs behind the banister who you can take out from outside. After the area you can see is fairly clear and your team is in position, press backspace to order your team to enter and clear. You must be on the south (left) wall to initiate the takedown. As before, wait for them to use a flashbang, then move in. Pay special attention to the door in the southwest corner and the southern stairs. Enemy reinforcements come from these directions.

TIP *While clearing out the small rooms on the first floor, use the shotgun to save CAR-15 ammo. The shotgun can take out two or three enemies who are close together.*

Clear the ground floor one room at a time.

Once you clear the entry lobby, clear the rest of the ground floor. Activate your night-vision goggles and head through the northwest door first. Move through a series of small rooms, clearing each as you go. You eventually come to a dead end. Pick up the first-aid kit in one of the rooms, then return to the main lobby. Now enter and clear the room through the southwest door. You may attempt to order your team to clear these rooms so that they use the proper entry techniques and their flashbangs. However, the militia tend to rush out of the other rooms, which makes this difficult. Take cover in an alcove in the south corner, by the doorway. Eliminate the two militia, collect the ammo and use it as a sniper position as enemies run out of the opposing doorways. There are several small rooms that you must check and clear of all enemies. Locate a flight of stairs that lead to the second level of the building. Once the ground level is clear, take the stairs to the top.

You now have to clear the second level. Usually, a couple militia are near the top of the stairs, so be ready. Move around, clearing out rooms as you go. Most of the rooms are empty, which gives you time to catch a breath. One of the rooms on the right, which is well lit, contains Delta Team 2 and their hostages. Don't rush in and kill them. Advance until all rooms in the building are clear.

Take out any militia in the hallway or who may be in the bedrooms after stunning them with flashbangs.

5. Rendezvous with Delta Team Two and the captured Tier Ones at waypoint Romeo.

Once the target building is clear, return to the room containing Delta Team 2. Your job is to provide cover fire as they move the hostages.

Meet up with Delta Team 2.

6. Select an M60 from the armory and move to the roof to cover Team Two's exfil.

At the armory, you can select a new weapon. Take the M60. You will need the heavy firepower over the long-range accuracy of a sniper rifle.

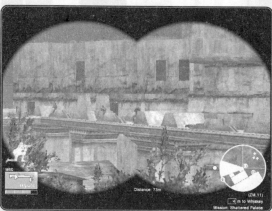

Use the binoculars to locate concentrations of militia overlooking the courtyard.

You need to take out the militia on the rooftops to the southeast first.

Then concentrate on the enemies to the east in the building across the street since that is where Team Two is headed.

Follow your orders and trade in the CAR-15 for an M60 from the armory. Near the stairway you climbed to the second level, you find more stairs leading to the roof. Quickly get your team to the roof. When you reach the roof, head to the eastern edge and engage the militia. Almost all are located on the rooftops or high walkways to the east and southeast. There is no time for accuracy and conserving ammo, so open fire. Start with the snipers in the windows to your right. Then quickly run to the other side of the roof and deal with the 3-4 militia stationed across the way. Now move to the center of the roof and begin to sweep slowly right to left. This will increase your accuracy somewhat. Do not shoot down into the courtyard as only friendlies are down there. Remember, you are not in danger, they are, so you do not need to worry about gunfire coming your way.

7. Exfil on Little Bird at waypoint X-Ray.

Once Delta Team 2 has successfully crossed the courtyard, you receive your orders to exfiltrate the area. Shortly thereafter, a Little Bird arrives and lands on the rooftop. Lead your team to the helo to complete the mission. Attach to the skid and you are out of there.

The Little Bird arrives to take your team to safety.

DIPLOMATIC IMMUNITY

BRIEFING

OPORD. 8-93, TFR

Date Time: 241430 September 93

1. Situation

In an attempt to free members of their clan, Habr Gedir militia forces have attacked a UN compound in Mogadishu. The enemy forces have taken control of the building, freed their compatriots, and are holding a number of UN hostages.

- Weather: Clear, hot.
- Terrain: Urban—walled compound.
- Enemy: Estimated 25–60 Habr Gedir militia equipped with small arms and RPGs. Some militia may be hiding among the hostages—secure for later identification.

2. Mission

- Who: Delta Teams 2-1 and 5-1, Ranger 4-2.

- What: Insert by helo. Locate and secure the hostages. All units return to base.
- When: Immediately after briefing.

3. Execution

- Commander's Intent: Rescue hostages, avoid civilian casualties.
- Concept of Operation: Both teams will insert directly into the courtyard of the compound. Delta 5-1 will assault and secure the courtyard and target building while Delta 2-1 locates the hostages. Once the hostages are secured, Ranger 4-2 will arrive with the extraction convoy.
- Coordinating Instructions: Delta 5-1 will lead the assault on the building. Ranger 4-2 will maintain distance from target until hostages are secure.

4. Service and Support

- Basic Load: CAR-15, Colt .45, Claymore.

Summary of Mission

A number of captured Habr Gadir were being transferred to UNOSOM II when there was an attack by a large number of militia gunmen. A small riot has ensued, and a number of UN personnel are being held hostages. Your team is being sent in to rescue them.

Suggested Loadout

Primary Weapon: CAR-15

Secondary Weapon: Colt .45

Accessory: Claymore

TACTICS

1. Defend the Little Birds. Take out the RPGs!

Your team approaches the compound from the air.

the skid seats of an AH-6 Little Bird. Hold on tight and make sure your rifle is ready for action. Keep it set at the default automatic fire mode. Your chopper is headed to the compound where the hostages are being held. Because the militia know that the Americans or the UN will send someone to rescue the hostages, you are expected.

When the mission begins, your team is flying on

2. Clear the ground floor of hostiles and secure the hostages.

As you fly past the main building, take out as many militia as possible.

As you approach the compound, your chopper will start taking small-arms fire. Militiamen below also start firing RPGs up at you. Because the chopper is moving quickly over the landscape, it is hard to draw a bead on a small target below, let alone hit something. You order the pilot to slow down and maintain a hover so you can engage the militia. Target enemies armed with an RPG before they can shoot down your Little Bird.

When the chopper slows to a hover, concentrate your fire on the RPG militia below. Just be careful —while hovering, the chopper is a sitting duck.

Head for the front door of the building in the compound.

As you circle the compound, clear the area outside the bordering walls. Most of the RPG militia are just outside these walls. Take some shots at the enemy inside the compound as well. If your Little Bird manages to survive the RPG attacks, it will set down in the courtyard. Hop off and move toward the building's front door.

A frag grenade thrown through the front door does a good job of clearing the room.

You come across a few enemies in the courtyard. Deal with them quickly and continue to waypoint Alpha in the lobby of the target building. As you approach, throw a frag grenade and through the front door. Switch back to your CAR-15 and rush in as soon as the grenade explodes. The hostages are in a room off to the right; the second Delta team will rescue them while you continue to clear the building.

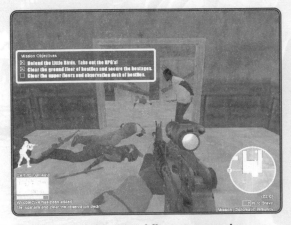

After clearing the ground floor, you receive a new objective.

3. Clear the upper floors and observation deck of hostiles.

Rush up the stairs to the upper level of the building.

While the second Delta team secures the hostages, take your team upstairs and go after the militia on the upper floors. In the large back room on the first floor is a first-aid kit. Once you get to the stairs, you can take them all the way to the top—usually without any resistance. However, you can expect at least one militia in the room at the top of the stairs and several in an adjacent room.

A frag grenade works wonders for clearing out the second room. Wait until it detonates before rushing in to make sure all militia there have been neutralized. Once this room is clear, you should get a new objective. If you don't, look up through the passageway in the ceiling to locate any remaining militia and take them out. Then hustle up the ladder.

Another frag grenade will clear out the room with the ladder.

4. Man the .50 cal on the roof. Defend the compound from militia counter attack.

Get to the .50-caliber machinegun as fast as you can.

A large force of militia is headed your way, and you are the only means of defending the compound from assault. Do not let those two technicals enter the compound.

By now the entire building is secure. However, the Habr Gadir are sending reinforcements to deal with you. Rush over to the .50-caliber machinegun mounted on the rooftop and get ready for a big firefight. Several technicals are headed your way, approaching from the west. Although the machineguns mounted on these vehicles are a threat, your primary concern is RPG militia. They are on foot across the paved street from the compound, to the north and south of the dirt road that runs perpendicular to the street. You may have to use the binoculars to spot them, but don't spend too much time gazing away. Eliminate them with bursts from your machinegun, then lay into the technicals.

TIP *While manning the machinegun on the rooftop, maintain a constant stream of fire. There is no need for you to stop firing. Lay down a wall of lead to keep all enemies away from the compound.*

---

5. Extract team and hostages to the evacuation convoy.

Don't forget to pick up the ammo by the gate.

After you have neutralized the militia assault from the west, it is time to get everybody out of Dodge. Lead your team back down the ladder and the stairway to the ground floor. Exit through the back door on the east side of the building. The second Delta team is waiting just outside with the hostages. Rush past them to the eastern gate of the compound. Pick up the ammo near the gate.

Take up a position at the gate, but do not yet leave the walled compound. Individual militia begin heading your way from the north and east. Deal with them until there is a lull, then move through the gate and east into the small courtyard on your way to waypoint Foxtrot. Your job is to secure a way to the Rangers and protect the hostages. The eastern gate of the compound is one of the most dangerous spots on your route to the Rangers.

Take out the militia headed toward the eastern gate as they appear in your sights.

Watch out for RPG militia on the rooftops.

Enemies lurk down many of the alleys, waiting to ambush you as you move past.

While your team stays behind, advance toward Foxtrot. Watch for enemies down alleyways as well as an RPG militia on the rooftop just to the north of Foxtrot. By the time you arrive at Foxtrot, the other Delta team—following your path—will begin moving with the hostages. Stay ahead of them. Although you will run across some enemies on the ground, the RPG militia on the rooftops are the real danger to the hostages and both Delta teams. One RPG round can kill many troops at once. Therefore, as you advance on to waypoint Hotel, keep your eyes up and constantly scanning 360 degrees so your force is not ambushed from above.

TIP *Watch your GPS map. As soon as the second Delta team and hostages have left the compound and are in the small courtyard, order your team to regroup and follow you. They will fall in behind the hostages and form a rear guard as they advance toward you.*

As you approach Hotel, the Rangers in the convoy start to drive toward you. Maintain a secure perimeter around Hotel until all the hostages arrive. When the convoy arrives, the mission is complete.

The Ranger convoy begins to move toward you. Just hold out a bit longer, and you will make it.

SHORE PATROL

BRIEFING

OPORD: 9-93, TFR

Date Time: 011900 October 93

1. Situation

Aidid has taken control of a radio transmitter in Habr Gedir territory, near the Mogadishu docks, and is using it to coordinate attacks on UN relief efforts. Multiple guards protect the area and the shoreline has been mined.

- **Weather: Clear, hot, low clouds, dim light.**
- **Terrain: Port area, docks, coastline, warehouses.**
- **Enemy: Unknown. Minimum 40-50 militia with shoulder arms.**

2. Mission

- **Who: Delta Team 5, 2 Ranger Chalks.**
- **What: Insert by local boat. Destroy radio equipment, return to base.**
- **When: 1900 hours, dusk.**

3. Execution

- **Commander's Intent: Destroy radio station's transmitting capabilities.**
- **Concept of Operation: Your team will board a local fishing boat and make a beach insertion. Locate and destroy radio equipment. Extraction will be by Little Bird at the docks. Two Ranger chalks on board helos will be available for contingencies. If the cargo ship is docked, it is a target of opportunity.**

4. Service and Support

- **Basic Load: CAR-15, Shotgun, Satchel Charges.**

Summary of Mission

Land on the beach and move to the building with the radio tower, where you will need to destroy the equipment inside. Then move to the shore to provide support for 2 Ranger chalks where you will receive further orders.

Suggested Loadout

Primary Weapon: CAR-15

Secondary Weapon: Shotgun

Accessory: Satchel charge

TACTICS

1. Land on beach.

The boat ride to the beach is the easiest part of the mission.

In this mission you must be very careful to protect your teammates. If you lose too many of them during combat, you will fail the mission. It is a good idea to save after the larger firefights. You begin on a local fishing boat. Prepare for combat immediately. Take out your binoculars and scan the beach ahead. That is where you will land. You see a number of red stakes all across the shoreline; this is a minefield. Right from the start, your mission appears to be quite a bit more complicated than planned. Snipe the two militia on the beach who begin firing at the boat.

2. Successfully navigate the minefield.

After hitting the beach, move southwest through this gap in the rocks.

Now head due north toward another gap in some rocks, then on to the buildings.

As the boat reaches shore, mortars start bombarding the beach. Jump down from the boat and get moving. You cannot worry about the mortars; there really is nothing you can do about them. Instead, concentrate on the minefield. Head due west, then turn southwest and move through a gap in some rocks. When you reach an area of blackened earth, turn due west and continue until you come across a gap in the mines that leads north. At each set of rocks, stop and wait for your teammates. This should prevent them from stepping near a mine. Follow this path north until you reach some buildings.

TIP *For most of this mission, use your night-vision goggles. They reveal militia hiding in the shadows around and inside buildings. Otherwise, you may not realize enemies are nearby until they start shooting. Also use binoculars to scout the area ahead at a distance so you can prepare for what lies ahead.*

3. Make your way to the radio tower.

Take out the militia among the buildings.

A few militia, including one carrying an RPG, hide around the buildings. Take them all out, then continue north into the area between the buildings. Before long, you run into more mines. Turn west and head up a rise following your waypoints to grid ZK,27. From this point you can see the radio tower on top of the target building to the northwest. However, there is no direct way there. Take out the large group of militia to your southwest and then head in that direction.

4. Make your way to the radio tower.

You must move north toward an open area.

Head through this alley by the shipping container.

Watch out for enemies along the way.

The only way to the radio tower requires you to move through the maze of buildings. Head south to an open area between buildings. Militia are at the south, east, and southwest parts of this open area. Take them all out, then head southwest through a passageway by a large shipping container. Take a right to head southwest for a bit, then turn left and continue northwest. Turn right again and move east across a small courtyard. Your commander tells you about a cargo ship and a future target. From there, head in a generally northern direction. All during this time, you must be ready to take out any enemies you encounter, but avoid shooting civilians—even though they may throw rocks at you. Eventually, as you continue north, you see the building with the radio tower on top.

5. Destroy the radio equipment.

Take out the militia hiding to the sides of the large doorway.

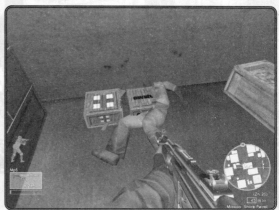

Pick up some ammo and a first-aid kit.

Several militia guard your way to the radio tower. Watch for them on the ground and on rooftops. There is a militia with an RPG directly behind you on the roof. Shoot the militia in front of the large container, then enter the container and use it as cover to take out the machinegunner. Once you reach the building, you will find a large doorway in the south side of the building. This is your way in. Two militia are in this first room: one to the right of the large doorway and the other to the left. Take them both out by leaning into the doorway, then head through a smaller doorway into the interior of the building. Down the first hallway as you approach a ramp leading up to the control room, you find a small room to the left. Take out the enemy inside, then pick up some ammo and a first-aid kit.

Order your team to rush in and clear the control room.

The flashbang stuns everyone inside.

Continue to the top of the ramps. Be ready for a militia at the doorway leading out to an open area, as well as another outside the door and to the right. The control room is to the left. Once your team is in place, press backspace to order them to enter and clear the room. First, one member of your team throws a flashbang. After it detonates and stuns everyone in the control room, your team automatically enters and clears the room.

6. Make your way to the pier.

Your new objective is to return to the shore. Time to get moving again. Continue through the back room, then down some stairs that lead to a large room in the eastern part of the building. A couple of militia are at ground level. You can shoot the one by the door from your position on the staircase. Once you eliminate them, you can expect several more militia to enter through a door to the west.

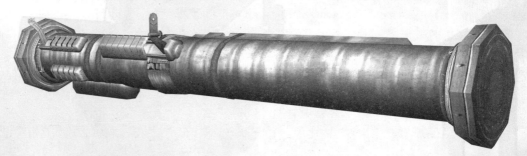

Exit the building and head for the ship.

Your team approaches the compound from the air.

After all militia have been neutralized, lead your team outside. Once again, you must navigate a maze to your next objective. You can expect enemies all along the way. Advance northeast to grid ZK,25. There is a first-aid kit behind the shack on your left here. Keep following the waypoints. Turn left and head west, then head northwest to a small alley at grid ZL,24. Move south for a short while before turning left. Follow the alleyway around, making three right turns followed by a left turn. Not only must you worry about civilians along this route (as well as occasional militia), but there is a militia on the rooftop and three that run up behind your team about halfway through this section. Move slowly and cautiously; there is no need to hurry.

Head down the slope toward the dock area.

You eventually come to a courtyard area. Move east across it, clearing as you go, then head southeast to grid ZJ,25, where you find more ammo and a first-aid kit behind a shack. At this point, take out some militia coming at you from the north, then descend the slope to the docks and head toward grid ZI,26. Again, you must move through some narrow gaps between buildings and eliminate several enemies. Eventually, you reach the main dock at the northwest corner of grid ZI,26.

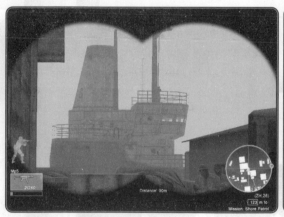

Use the binoculars to get a view of the ship.

Use long-range fire to take out the militia on the pier.

As soon as you near the pier, you need to take out the militia on the .50 cal straight ahead. After that, immediately turn 90-degrees to your left and eliminate the other .50 cal gunner.

7. Destroy the cargo that was unloaded from the ship.

Race back to the first .50 cal and lay down some serious lead. Rangers will begin to fast-rope from 2 Black Hawks. Continue to provide cover fire. After all resistance is eliminated, destroy the cargo to the north, about eight stacks of crates.

Take out militia on the ship as you approach it.

Throw the satchel charges down into the hold.

As soon as you board the ship. Order your entire team to hold at the end of the pier while you board the ship alone. They cover your rear while you get ready to destroy the ship. Once you have climbed up the gangplank, turn right, toward the bow, and take out a militia hiding in wait. Now walk over to the open hatch leading down into the cargo hold. Don't climb down the ladder. Instead, pull out a satchel charge and throw it down into the hold. Now it is time to get off the ship.

8. Get on the Little Bird and detonate your satchel charge.

Descend the gangplank and head for the Little Bird. Attach to the Little Bird and lift off. Select the detonator and blow up the ship. After the explosion and the sinking of the ship, the mission ends as a success.

The ship is destroyed.

IRENE

BRIEFING

OPORD: 10-93, TFR

Date Time: 031535 October 93

1. Situation

Two of Aidid's high-ranking officers will be meeting with other militia members today near the Olympic Hotel in the heart of Habr Gedir territory.

- **Weather: Clear, hot.**
- **Terrain: Urban, city center.**
- **Enemy: Estimated 500 Habr Gedir militia equipped with small arms and RPGs. Technicals with .50-caliber mounted weapons.**
- **Friendly: None.**

2. Mission

- **Who: Ranger Platoons 1-4, 160th, Delta Teams 1-5.**
- **What: Insert by helo, locate and secure principals. All units return to base.**
- **When: To be determined based on intel. NLT sunset.**

3. Execution

- **Commander's Intent: Secure the target building and capture Aidid's officers.**
- **Concept of Operation: Chalks and Delta will make an aerial assault on the target building. Chalks will secure the four corners while the Delta Teams make their assault from the roof. 4th Platoon drivers will bring extraction vehicles to the Area of Operations (AO) once the principals are secure. All units will extract to base via ground vehicles.**

4. Service and Support

- **Basic Load: CAR-15, Shotgun, AT4.**

PRIMA'S OFFICIAL STRATEGY GUIDE

Summary of Mission

This is our best chance to capture two of Aidid's top lieutenants and a number of lower-level officers. This mission will include four chalks of Rangers, Delta assault teams, and multiple SOAR helicopters. We should be in and out in less than 30 minutes.

Suggested Loadout

Primary Weapon: CAR-15

Secondary Weapon: Shotgun

Accessory: AT4

TACTICS

1. Board the waiting MH-6 Little Bird.

You begin the mission at Mogadishu Airport—the base for Task Force Ranger.

Hop aboard this Little Bird and get ready for a ride into the city.

This is one of the most difficult missions yet. In fact, it is the first in a series of five linked missions. Although the action is concentrated into specific areas, it is intense. Keep your magazine full and be ready for anything. You begin the mission at Mogadishu Airport, the headquarters for Task Force Ranger (TFR). At the start, follow your waypoint onto the tarmac where a number of helicopters wait. You will be riding on a landing skid seat of a Little Bird.

The Little Bird ride takes time, but is cool to watch from an external view.

Take out the RPG militia below.

The target building is ahead.

The Little Birds carry in the Delta Teams while the Ranger chalks take the Black Hawks. Once aboard the Little Bird, sit back and enjoy the ride. You will fly over the ocean, then on toward the main part of Mogadishu. As you approach the city, bring your rifle up to the scope view and aim ahead and down. Civilians are below, so watch your fire. Your targets are a number of militia armed with RPGs, which they fire at the helicopters. If an RPG hits your helo, the mission is over for you.

2. Storm the target building and eliminate resistance.

Wait for your team to dismount, then head for the stairway.

Drop the militia at the bottom of the stairs.

As the Little Bird swoops to the target building, get ready to hop off. After it touches down, dismount and head for the doorway leading from the rooftop to the third floor. The stairs go down, and left. Strafe around the corner where the stairs turn and take out the enemy below and behind a partition in the doorway. Another enemy walks around near the base of the stairs, so watch for him and neutralize this threat.

Prepare to order your team to clear the room on the right.

Watch for militia coming up the stairs.

When you reach the bottom of the stairs, expect more trouble. Rather than stopping at the base, continue running straight ahead from the stairs and into the area behind the partition. From here, load your weapon, and clear out the room to your immediate right. Throw a flashbang in to stun the militia inside. Stack up your team at the doorway, then order your team to enter and clear. Rush in and take down the militia. You receive a message that the third floor is clear. After it is clear, turn around and be ready for the enemy coming up the stairs. Another message informs you when the floor below is clear.

5. Secure the Tier One prisoners on the second floor.

Clear this room, but do not hit the Tier One officials.

It is now time to take the stairs down to the second floor. Although it looks clear, the Tier One personnel and their guards are behind some locked steel doors. This is a job for a grenade. Toss it, jump back and prepare to breach the doors. While the smoke is clearing, switch to your rifle and run along the wall so you are positioned to the left of the door. Be ready for militia who might run out. Throw a flashbang inside.

The room is clear—deal with those enemies in the room on the right.

Once it detonates, move across the doorway, then enter the room so your right shoulder is against a wall as you face into the room. You want to take the lieutenants inside alive, so shoot only militia carrying weapons while they are stunned. Putting on night-vision goggles at this point will help prevent you from accidentally shooting the prisoners. Watch out for the long room that connects on the right. The militia in there will not be stunned by the flashbang, so, while your team is clearing the main room with the tier-ones, throw another flashbang into the side room and rush in to clear it.

4. Get the prisoners to the convoy.

Lead your prisoners downstairs toward the door.   **Don't forget the first-aid kit and ammo.**

With the guards neutralized, you receive a new order to bring the prisoners downstairs to the convoy. Lead the way down and straight out the door to the waiting convoy if you are unharmed. However, if you have taken damage, head to the room south of the door on the first floor to find a first-aid kit and some ammo. Load up and continue outside to the convoy.

Continue outside to the convoy.

5. Help Ranger Chalk 4 repel the enemy.

Turn this alley into a kill zone.

Chalk 4 is secure.

When you reach the convoy, you learn that Chalk 4 is taking heavy fire and needs assistance. Lead your team north to an alley that continues north. After picking up the ammo, your rifle is fully loaded. As you reach the alley, a number of militia come, headed for the convoy. Take out all of them—especially the RPG enemies, who will either fire at your team or the Ranger chalk. Watch for additional militia that race around the southern corner of the building. With the alley clear, head toward the chalk at waypoint Foxtrot and clear the area. You will immediately come under fire from all directions. Put your back against the building so you face the chalk and open fire to your right. Then peek around the building and take out two more RPG gunners.

6. Help Ranger Chalk 2 repel the enemy.

Head toward the target building.

Chalk 2 is ahead.

Take out the enemies as they round the corner.

Once the area is secure, you receive orders to help Chalk 2. To get to waypoint Golf, head south, then east, running past the target building. The alleys that you run through will quickly fill with enemies. Take them out with an emphasis on those militia carrying RPGs. If you drop prone, you are less likely to be shot.

7. Secure the perimeter.

Go the machinegun at waypoint Hotel.

Mow down any militia who come into your sights.

When you repel this attack, you receive another order. More militia are coming from the east and southeast. You must take up a position behind a .50-caliber machinegun mounted on a wrecked technical at waypoint Hotel. You must get that machinegun firing as soon as you can run to it. Clear the area between the two buildings east of you. Pan to the right to take on groups of militia coming at you from the southeast. Keep up the pressure, firing at one area, then the next.

Black Hawk Super Six One takes a hit and goes down.

As you deal with these human waves, Black Hawks and Little Birds orbit your position. One of the Black Hawks, Super Six One, takes a hit from an RPG and goes down to the southeast of your position. This quick and easy mission just dramatically changed. Instead of returning to base as your orders previously stated would happen following nabbing the prisoners, the mission ends—to be continued during the next mission in the campaign.

LOST CONVOY

BRIEFING

OPORD: 10-93, TFR

Date Time: 031745 October 93

1. Situation

Super Six One has been hit by an RPG and has gone down northeast of the target building. We have to get men to that position ASAP.

- Weather: Clear, hot.
- Terrain: Urban, city center.
- Enemy: Estimated 500 Habr Gedir militia equipped with small arms and RPGs. Technicals with .50-caliber mounted weapons.
- Friendly: None.

2. Mission

- Who: Delta 5-1, Ranger 4-2.
- What: Move by convoy to crash site, provide security and first aid.
- When: Immediately.

3. Execution

- Commander's Intent: Get a team of men to the crash site. Assess the wounded and secure the area until extraction can be made.
- Concept of Operation: Use the extraction convoy to get close to the crash site. Move the rest of the way on foot and set up a secure perimeter.

4. Service and Support

- Basic Load: M21, Colt .45, Claymore.

Summary of Mission

Super Six One has been hit by an RPG and went down northeast of the target building. Take the convoy to the crash site and secure it. We need to get a team there before the Habr Gedir overrun the position.

Suggested Loadout

Primary Weapon: M21

Secondary Weapon: Colt .45

Accessory: Claymore

TIP *During the middle phase of this mission, while advancing on foot, you will wish you had brought along a CAR-15. However, no matter how tough it may be, take the M21. The last phase of the mission requires a sniper rifle, and if you don't take it with you, you will be hurting when you get to the crash site.*

TACTICS

1. Protect the convoy from enemy militia while en route to the crash site.

This mission starts with you manning a machinegun in the lead Humvee.

Clear out the area behind the target building as you drive past. The militia here can wreak havoc on your convoy.

This is another tough mission. After defending the perimeter around the target building in the previous mission, you saw a Black Hawk go down. Now you must lead a convoy to the crash site. You will man the .50-caliber machinegun in the lead Humvee. Although you may have a lot of firepower at your command, you are a sitting duck for every militia sniper and rifleman between the target building and the crash site.

Watch for RPG militia on the rooftops.

You must fire both high and low as you drive along the streets of Mogadishu.

Although the militia soldiers with rifles can cause you some serious hurt, the real threat you face is from RPGs. The militia carrying these can be at street level or up on the rooftops. You can take several hits of rifle fire and continue, but if an RPG hits your Humvee, the mission is over. Therefore, you really must keep your eyes open and looking for RPG militia before they can fire. Use your binoculars to scan ahead to locate RPG militia, then engage them with the machinegun. In fact, because you are just going along for the ride, keep a finger poised over Ⓑ to quickly bring up the binocular view and then return to normal view to shoot.

Watch for civilians and avoid shooting them.

Mogadishu is a fairly populous city. Not everyone along the route is militia, so use caution when firing. If you kill too many innocent civilians, the mission will end in failure. Remember that you are here to help these people. What makes this difficult is the fact that the militia look very similar to the civilians. Just look before you shoot, using the binoculars to get a closer view at groups of people from a distance. As for people above the street level—they are all militia, so shoot away.

Snipers hide in the open windows on either side of the roads.

Take out this pair of technicals ASAP.

During some areas of the drive, you move through narrow streets with tall buildings on either side. If the windows are opened—not shuttered closed—be on the lookout for snipers. In many cases, you cannot see them until you actually drive past, so keep traversing the gun back and forth. Other enemies you face during your drive to the crash site include machinegun positions and technicals. As soon as you see either, target them and fire until they are taken out. They can cause a lot of damage to your convoy and you.

TIP *The distance to the crash site is not that far—as the bird flies. However, the militia have set up several roadblocks, which require your convoy to take detours so you cover much more distance than first expected. Luckily, you have quite a few save spots. Use them as needed, especially prior to tough spots that may require a few attempts to pass. Just be sure to save at least two spots for the part of the mission where you are on foot.*

2. Dismount from the Humvee and move out the crash site on foot.

3. Move to the crash site on foot.

Pick up this first-aid kit. You will probably need it.

After driving around for a while and not finding a way for the convoy to reach the crash site, you are ordered to dismount and head the rest of the way on foot. By this time, you are probably wounded from fire taken during the drive. Instead of heading south toward waypoint Bravo, run straight ahead. Here you will find a first-aid kit, but beware of the militia standing near it. Pick it up and continue following the waypoints. Another first-aid kit is hidden just inside a building at grid D,-10 if you need it.

Keep your sniper rifle at the ready.

Don't even worry about switching to scope view for enemies who are fairly close.

As you advance to the crash site, remember that you are carrying a sniper rifle. The M21 is semiautomatic, but has a much lower rate of fire than the M16 or CAR-15 in semiautomatic mode. You must aim carefully to make sure you hit an enemy with the first shot. Unlike the assault rifles, you cannot walk with the sniper rifle in scope view. Instead, just keep it at the ready as you weave your way through the alleys. If you see an enemy at close range, just take him out. However, if the enemy is at medium to long range, take the quick second to switch to scope view, center him in the crosshairs, and then take him out. You can also switch to prone or crouch, before switching to sniper mode, to make yourself less of a target.

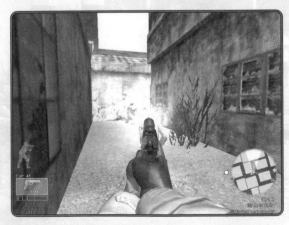

The pistol works great for taking out enemies as you move through the narrow alleys.

Because the sniper rifle is somewhat awkward while moving though narrow alleys where you could easily come upon a couple militia, try using the Colt .45, or whatever secondary weapon you are carrying for dealing with enemies at close range. Don't forget that you can back up to hide around a corner if you happen upon trouble. There is no reason you have to stay and fight it out right then. Instead, withdraw a bit and throw a frag grenade around the corner. Then peek around to finish off any remaining or stunned enemies.

Use the sniper scope view to take out militia at long range and for clearing open areas before moving through them.

Whenever you come to a large or open area you must cross or move through, take some time to scout it out from a safe corner with cover. Pick off as many enemies as possible with the sniper rifle to secure the area before continuing on to the next waypoint. The last thing you want to happen is to get out in the middle of an open area and be shot at from many directions. Don't forget to check windows and rooftops for snipers.

4. Setup a sniping position, overlooking the crash site, on the roof of the bombed out building.

You have reached the bombed-out building. Now to find the stairs.

Climb up this ladder to the third floor.

As you approach waypoint Foxtrot, you receive a new objective. The crash site is under attack from advancing militia. Instead of rushing in and getting caught in the assault, you are to head to a bombed-out building. The waypoints lead you right to it. The stairway can be somewhat tough to find because it is partially covered in rubble. Just jump up onto the rubble, then take the stairs to the second floor. Go up the ladder to the third floor. There you will find some ammo and a first-aid kit.

The crash site is below.

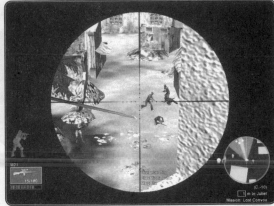

Take out the militia nearest the Black Hawk first.

The downed Black Hawk is below you and to the east. Take up a position at a window and begin helping to secure the crash site. The militia come at the crash from the north, east, and south, so use the scope view and start picking them off. You usually don't have to worry about taking any fire; the militia are in a frenzy because they are trying to reach the crash and the survivors there. A good tactic is to start at the crash site and work your way outward from it. This lets you take out those militia who are the greatest threat first, then help keep others away.

5. Take out all RPG militia on buildings surrounding the crash site.

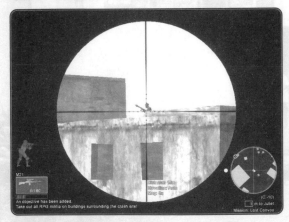

The RPG militia are waiting on the rooftops.

A C-SAR helo is coming in to drop off a rescue team. However, the militia are counting on this and waiting. They have positioned several RPG militia on rooftops around the crash site so they can shoot down a second Black Hawk. Your new objective is to clear the rooftops and provide a safe drop zone. As soon as you receive this order, take a break from shooting the enemies at ground level and start looking for RPG militia on the rooftops. Take out each and every one to meet this objective. Once the rooftops are clear, check the ground level for any more RPGs that may be hiding.

6. Defend those soldiers at the crash site until they can be evacuated.

VALIANT SOLDIER

BRIEFING

OPORD: 10-93, TFR

Date Time: 031800 October 93

1. Situation

Another Black Hawk, Super 64, was hit by an RPG and went down south of the target building. We can't get them on the radio. A group of Rangers and the Combat Search-and-Rescue (C-SAR) has secured the first site, but there is not a second C-SAR available. We have men scattered throughout the area radioing in trying to link up.

- **Weather: Clear, hot.**
- **Terrain: Urban, city center.**
- **Enemy: Estimated 500 Habr Gedir militia equipped with small arms, grenades, RPGs. Technicals with .50-caliber mounted weapons.**
- **Friendly: None.**

2. Mission

- **Who: Delta Team 5.**

- **What: Move by foot, link up with scattered units, move to the crash site.**
- **When: Immediately.**

3. Execution

- **Commander's Intent: Link up with scattered soldiers. Get to second crash site.**
- **Concept of Operation: Move to the second crash site on foot while linking with any stragglers you can find. Once you have enough firepower, get to that helo before the Habr Gedir capture or kill the survivors.**

4. Service and Support

- **Basic Load: CAR-15-203, Colt .45, AT4.**

Summary of Mission

There's been another Black Hawk shot down. Super 64 was hit by an RPG and crashed south of the target building. We also have men separated from their units. Collect a team and make your way to the second crash site.

Suggested Loadout

Primary Weapon: CAR-15-203

Secondary Weapon: Colt. 45

Accessory: AT4

TACTICS

1. Rendezvous with the soldier at waypoint Charlie.

TIP *This can be a tough mission. Save your progress often. Remember, you have a lot of saves for this mission, so use them. There are several places you won't want to go through twice if you can avoid it.*

You start in a ruined building. Don't worry, you are leaving quickly.

When the mission begins, it is just you and another Delta Operator. You must move through a very hostile Mogadishu on your own, linking up with stragglers on your way to the second crash site. The immediate area around where you begin is clear. However, don't expect that to last long—especially once you start moving.

Stay close to the wall on your right as you head to Bravo.

Follow waypoints through the city, but do not feel that you must blindly stay on the line showing the most direct route to the next waypoint. Instead, take time every so often to switch to the full-screen map view and see if you can find a good route that provides as much cover and concealment as possible. Moving to waypoint Alpha is pretty easy. You will not face much resistance. However, from Alpha to Charlie (your first objective), you must cross some large open areas. As you move west through grid ZW,-9, hug the wall to the left all the way around and watch for militia directly ahead. Get to the short walled area in front of you, which you can use for cover before heading on to the building with the first soldier.

Clear the streets around Charlie.

You have located the first soldier. Time to head to the next group.

Waypoint Charlie is in grid ZV,-8 with the soldier in a building completely surrounded by a road. There are two entrances into this building. It does not matter which entrance you choose. Locate one, take out any militia who might shoot at you during your advance, then make a break for the building. Link up with the lone soldier holding out there and get ready to continue. There is a first aid kit at the top of the stairs if you need it.

TIP *If any soldiers in your team are hit and wounded, they will not be able to keep up with you if you run. Their wounds also make them more susceptible to enemy fire because they cannot move as quickly through open areas. Watch out for your team. Order the team to hold in a safe spot while you advance to scout enemy positions or take out a sniper. Once the area is clear, order your team to regroup and follow.*

2. Rendezvous with soldiers on the top floor of the building at waypoint Juliet.

Use anything for cover as you head to waypoint Delta.

The next group of soldiers is at waypoint Juliet, but just reaching Delta can be tough. It is nearly 140 meters away from Charlie in a straight line, but you must move around buildings and through alleys as much as possible to keep your team safe. Start by heading north from the building where you picked up the soldier and move next to the buildings as you head west and then north again.

As you continue toward Echo, you can really use some alleys to cover your flanks. There is first aid located along the way at ZU,-6. Continue to waypoint Echo, a fairly large building in grid ZT,-4. You must cross a large open area to reach the building. However, instead of rushing straight to the building, circle to the east as you approach, using the shanties for cover. This will help protect your right flank and allow you to clear the open area as you move. You will need to take out the .50 cal before advancing to the building. After you do this, race through the opening by the .50 cal into the building.

Check alleys as you advance.

You have linked up with the second group of soldiers.

Watch out for civilians. The militia like to hide near them.

Once you enter the building, clear and secure the ground floor before heading upstairs. No enemies are on the second floor, so check your fire so you don't kill a friendly.

3. Rendezvous with soldier pinned by snipers in large building to the south at waypoint Papa.

This courtyard is filled with militia and surrounded by snipers in the upstairs windows.

Stay to the south and take out the snipers in the windows ahead of you.

Now it is time to head south toward waypoint Kilo. Beware of the militia that are now trying to occupy the first floor. You must move across the open area, so use all the cover you can find. When you begin moving toward waypoint Gulf, watch out for snipers in the upstairs windows of the buildings along your route. Use the binoculars to locate them, then either fire a grenade into the window or fire a burst from your rifle. As before, move along the line of buildings, this time on your left, rather than moving across another open area. Stay low and move slowly as you clear the militia that come running toward you. Stay close to the buildings on the south side, and be sure to clear the windows to the west directly ahead. You can use the little alcoves in the building for cover, then peek around the corner to take shots. You can also lie down behind wrecked cars and shoot from behind them. Eventually, you arrive at waypoint Papa, marked by a bus, to find another soldier and some much-needed ammo.

4. Rendezvous with Ranger 2-3 who is in a warehouse at waypoint Victor.

Take out the snipers above you.

Be very careful as you exit the building where the last soldier was hiding. En route to waypoint Quebec, you must move through a gauntlet of snipers. Consider ordering your team to hold while you advance to take out the snipers. As you move south, hug the wall to your left. The snipers are above you in the windows. Although they cannot shoot down at you from this position, you can shoot up and take them out. Move to the gun emplacement at the southern end of your movement, shooting anyone who gets in your way. Take control of the machinegun and clear out any remaining snipers and the streets to the north and west of your position. From this emplacement, you can fire at another machinegun emplacement to the west.

Use the machinegun to clear out this street and the snipers on the balcony.

Use the binoculars to locate enemies at long range.

As you advance to Romeo, take out the snipers above and to the north in the windows on the corner of a building. Then run across the street to the technical and lay down a mass of lead along the road to the north, being sure to hit the balcony up to the right as well. If you use binoculars, you can see a third wrecked technical at the end of the road to the north. Take out the gunner with some very long-range machinegun fire. Then, once the road is clear, order your team to fall in and head north. Stay to one side of the road. Where the building on the right ends and the area opens up to some small shacks, look to the east and take out the sniper on the roof before he starts taking potshots at your team.

Rush through this door to find the next soldier.

Waypoint Victor is directly ahead, but a large open area exists to the west of the building where the soldier is holed up. He will release a smoke flare to indicate his position. Clear this area before going for the soldier, because you must cross it later anyway. Take up a position along a corner of a building and then peek around the corner to engage the enemy. Once you have taken care of most of the resistance, rush for the building at Victor. The door will automatically open, allowing you to enter and retrieve ammo and first aid.

5. Rendezvous with Delta 5-3 who is pinned down to the northwest at waypoint Zulu.

Take up a position behind the low wall and use it as cover while clearing out the shantytown area.

It is safer to hop over this low wall than to move out into the street to go around it.

This is the last objective for the mission. Before you leave the building at waypoint Victor, make sure your weapon is loaded and you are ready for action. Move quickly as you exit. Use binoculars to locate militia on rooftops in the distance.

Head into this passage to reach the last group of soldiers.

Lead your team due west. You can hop over this low wall rather than expose yourself by going around it. Stay as far north as possible as you move west toward waypoint X-Ray. Head north to Yankee and duck inside a building on your way to Zulu and the last group of soldiers, where the mission ends.

You made it. However, it does not look like you will reach the downed helicopter anytime soon.

LAST STAND

BRIEFING

OPORD: 10-93, TFR

Date Time: 040600 October 93

1. Situation

Habr Gedir forces have overrun the second crash site. All crew are captured or killed. We are recalling all units back to base. Aerial recon shows an enemy mortar position near your location that will have to be eliminated to clear your exfiltration.

- Weather: Hazy, dim light, hot.
- Terrain: Urban—city center.
- Enemy: Estimated 500 Habr Gedir militia equipped with small arms, grenades, and RPGs. Technicals with .50-caliber mounted weapons.
- Friendly: None.

2. Mission

- Who: Delta Team 5.
- What: Eliminate mortars, get team out of Mogadishu center.
- When: Immediately.

3. Execution

- Commander's Intent: Return team safely to base.
- Concept of Operation: Aerial recon shows a mortar position pinning down your team. If you can circle behind it and plant a satchel charge, your team can safely get out.

4. Service and Support

- Basic Load: CAR-15/203, Colt .45, Satchel Charge.

Summary of Mission

Your team is being pinned down by a mortar position. You must get around behind it and take it out with a satchel charge. Once it's clear, your team will be able to return to base.

Suggested Loadout

Primary Weapon: CAR-15-203

Secondary Weapon: Colt .45

Accessory: Satchel charge

TACTICS

1. Exit the building and proceed to your waypoints.

Your position is not very good at the start.

Your squad is pinned down. If you leave the building in which you are holed up, the militia outside tears you apart. However, until those mortars are silenced, the convoy cannot reach you and take you to safety. Because you cannot make a frontal assault on the mortars, you must go around a back way.

Take out the sniper on the balcony.

From the place where you begin the mission, head south and then out through a hole in the wall. You pass by some other Delta Operators as you head to the first waypoint. Slow down and approach the back alley with caution. A couple of militia patrol the alley, and one is up on a balcony to your left. Take care of all of them, then head northeast down the alley.

2. Follow waypoints through the back streets to the objective.

Watch for the militia hiding behind the crates on top of this bus.

This sniper to the north can cause problems if you don't take him out early.

There is an enemy on top of a bus at the end of the alley. Use the binoculars to spot him, then take him out with your rifle. Once you reach the end of the alley, hop over a low wall. Turn right to take out an enemy, then advance as you make a slow turn to the left until you face north. Watch for enemies among the shacks. You also need to find a sniper up on the roof of a building due north. Drop him before he can shoot at your team. A militia is down a short alley to your right, and one is ahead behind a fire barrel. You may start taking fire from behind as well. If this happens, face the tall building to the south and fire up into the open windows to take out another sniper.

Take out the militia in this window as you head north.

A couple of Little Birds clear the way for you.

Continue following the waypoints north. When you are walking between some buildings, be ready to take out a sniper up in the window on your left. Night-vision goggles help you see snipers hiding in the shadows of dark windows. You come to a small courtyard area. Hug the walls and make your way around to the east. There are some militia in the courtyard and snipers on the roofs to the south of the area. As usual, take your time. If you rush across this courtyard area and down an alleyway to the east, you will run into a mounted machinegun position. However, if you advance carefully, clearing as you go, a couple of Little Birds show up and take out the machinegun position for you.

TIP *A first-aid kit is down a small alley leading south from the courtyard area.*

The Little Birds make short work of this militia concentration.

After the Little Birds help you, head down the alley to the east. More militia are in another open area near grid Z0,5. Neutralize them. Then head south, following your waypoints. At the southern end of this open area, expect more resistance, and more again when you turn east.

For the next bit, you just move through some narrow alleys heading in a northern direction. There is not a lot of trouble around here. However, be ready as you enter grid ZQ,5. A large group of militia is at grid ZQ,6. Don't engage them. Instead, wait for the Little Birds to show up again and eliminate a majority of the threat there. Get a front row seat for the fireworks by crouching behind the tires. Once the area has been bombarded, move north. Watch out for survivors, especially one off to the right and another on a rooftop to the northeast. Near a destroyed technical you can find a first-aid kit.

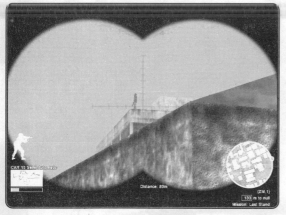

Another sniper on a rooftop.

Continue north to the end of this wide-open street. Your waypoints lead you west. Hold for a bit. When you turn around the corner, a sniper is up on a rooftop to the northwest. You need the binoculars to find him. However, be sure to take him out before continuing down the alleyway to the west. Advance cautiously, militia are ahead of you and off to the sides of the alleyway.

As you approach the southwest corner of grid ZP,7, look up and to the west to find another sniper on a rooftop. There is an RPG militia on a rooftop in grid ZN,7, so always look all around and up. After heading west for a ways, your waypoints turn you to the south. When they do, get ready for trouble. At the southern end of the alley, in grid ZN,6, you see an emplacement with a machinegun. Peek around the corner and fire a grenade down the alley to take out the militia manning the gun. Then head south to an open area off to the right.

Launch a grenade down the alley to take out a technical.

TIP *If you need some medical attention, pick up the first-aid kit by the technical.*

A militia with an RPG waits to ambush you from an upstairs window.

A first-aid kit and some sorely needed ammo.

When you reach the open area, turn right and hug the walls as you move west and then south. You will need to go west again, but be ready for more enemies up ahead. The open area around ZL,6 is crawling with militia. In addition, snipers waiting to ambush your team are on the rooftops and in several windows. Activate your night-vision goggles so you can see into the windows, then slowly cross this area. A good tactic is to find a position with some cover and look around from there using the binoculars. Locate any militia you can and neutralize them, then rush to another position of cover and do the same. A technical is in ZL,5, so take out the enemy on the gun, then move toward it. To the west of the technical, in some rubble, is a first aid kit and some more ammo. By this time, you probably need the ammo.

From the supplies, keep moving west. Before long, you must turn south again. This is the last leg of your round about path to the mortars, so get ready for some action. Hug the walls on your right as you move south. Watch for snipers on the buildings to the south as well as in the windows overlooking the mortar position. Slowly strafe left from behind corners of the buildings to engage one enemy at a time.

3. Eliminate enemy mortar crew.

The mortar position is well manned.

Launch a grenade or two to take out some of the militia.

Rush in to take out any remaining enemies near the mortars.

As soon as you can see the mortar position, duck back and ready a grenade in your launcher. Peek around the corner and take out the two snipers in the windows before advancing. Fire a grenade into the mortar position. You might even try throwing a flashbang into the position. Whatever method, or combination of methods, you choose, make a rush for the mortar position. Stay low in a crouch when you get there and clear out any remaining militia.

4. Destroy mortar position with satchel charges.

Place a satchel charge next to each of the two mortars.

Blow the charges!

Some militia fire at you from the southeast. However, your teammate should be able to deal with them. You need to take out snipers in buildings to the south. Once the mortar position is clear of enemies, get out the satchel charges. Place one next to each of the two mortars. A first-aid kit is in this area, so grab it if you need it. Move your team southwest of the mortars, then pull out your detonator and set off the charges.

5. Regroup with the rescue convoy at the pick-up point.

Run for the convoy. You don't want to be left behind.

With the mortars destroyed, the convoy can now come and pick you up. Once you see the convoy moving, head due east. This allows you to avoid most of the fire coming from the south. However, you need to deal with two remaining gun emplacements. Head south from the mortar area towards the wall. Just before you get there, turn to your right and snipe the militia behind the machinegun. Follow the wall around to destroy the last gun emplacement. When you get to the part of the road that runs north-south, run straight for the convoy. When you get near it, the mission is complete.

MOGADISHU MILE

BRIEFING

OPORD: 10-93, TFR

Date Time: 040715 October 93

1. Situation

We've got a rescue convoy in the area that will carry the wounded to a strongpoint we've established. We have security there, and it's in a friendly area of the city.

- **Weather: Hazy, dimly lit, hot.**
- **Terrain: Urban, city center.**
- **Enemy: Estimated 500 Habr Gedir militia equipped with small arms and RPGs. Technicals with .50-caliber mounted weapons.**
- **Friendly: None.**

2. Mission

- **Who: Delta 5.**
- **What: Load wounded onto trucks, provide security for convoy or follow to strongpoint.**
- **When: Immediately.**

3. Execution

- **Commander's Intent: Get everyone to base.**
- **Concept of Operation: The convoy will arrive at your location and load the wounded. If there is no room, follow on foot and use the trucks for cover. If they have to stop, provide security and/or clear any roadblocks.**

4. Service and Support

- **Basic Load: CAR-15/M203, Shotgun, AT4.**

Summary of Mission

A rescue convoy has been dispatched from base. When it arrives, load the wounded and follow it to a strongpoint we've established. Provide cover fire for the trucks and watch for snipers.

Suggested Loadout

Primary Weapon: CAR-15-203

Secondary Weapon: Shotgun

Accessory: AT4

TACTICS

1. Help protect the convoy from enemy fire.

This mission will be entirely on foot.

If you thought the missions were going to get any easier, think again. This is one long walk with enemies shooting at you from every direction. It is useful to know ahead of time which route the convoy will take to the stadium. Even though the stadium is due west of your starting point, the convoy must take a round about way to its destination because of roadblocks and buildings. It begins in grid I,11 and drives west to H,11 where it turns south. It continues south to G,1, then turns west. At C,1, it turns north, then heads east from C,3 to E,3. It heads north and west to the stadium at B,9.

Run ahead of the convoy to the corner of the wall.

Take out this RPG militia and other enemies as they walk out of the gateway.

As you move along with the convoy, use the APCs for cover. They block the small-arms fire from one of your flanks. The key is to know which side of the APC to be on! At the start of the mission, run out ahead of the convoy. Move due west to H,11, where the wall to your left comes to a corner. At this corner, face south and shoot any enemy who comes out of a gateway to the south. To the south is an RPG militia who fires RPGs at you. Locate him with the binoculars, then take him out. If you see an RPG headed your way, move behind the corner of the wall for protection. Although the APCs provide great protection, your job is to protect them, so you will need to step out to shoot militia. If an RPG gets through, the mission will be a failure.

Use this APC for cover.

After dealing with these enemies, cross the street to the right and follow the convoy south. Keep an APC on your left for cover from fire originating in the east. If you stay by the second APC in line, the first APC and lead Humvee will help clear your way for you. At grid H,9, the road makes a short jog to the west before continuing south. As you near this point, move away from the convoy and take cover near the buildings along the western side of the road. A machinegun position at G,7 opens, causing damage to your team if you are in the way. Watch out for militia to your right, but they are easier to deal with than the machinegun position. Just continue moving south.

2. Catch up to the convoy.

The convoy is speeding up and leaving you behind.

Once the convoy reaches G,7, it takes heavier fire from the enemy. As a result, it speeds up and leaves your team on foot behind. Not only do you no longer have the APCs for cover, but you also no longer benefit from the supporting fire of the vehicle-mounted machineguns. Head west into the small alleys between the buildings. There is a path in grid G,6 that allows you to move south parallel to the road. However, it will eventually force you back to the road.

You have not been abandoned. By the time you rejoin the road, a Little Bird calls in to tell you to keep your heads down. It makes a strafing run along the road. When it flies by, head south down the road and duck into a building on the west side. It is little more than a walkway leading south, but it provides great cover for a bit. In the walkway are a couple of militia. Take them out, then hold up here. From the south end of the walkway, use your binoculars to look down the street and see what is waiting. Bring up your rifle and take out as many enemies as possible. The Little Bird makes another strafing run, so stay put until it passes.

Take out enemies along the road from the cover at the end of the walkway.

Hug the walls of the buildings, using every alcove as cover while you advance.

Drop this militia in the alley.

Grab the first-aid kit and ammo here.

After clearing those militia you can see from the walkway, advance south. Hug the wall with your right shoulder and use the little alcoves in the wall for cover. Peek around the corners and check out the area to the south for enemies, then take them out before continuing. By the time you arrive at grid G,4, you can avoid the street by taking an alley west, then south to G,3. There is a militia in the alley and another at the end on a roof of a shack to the south. However, what you really want is the first-aid kit and ammo in the rubble to the east. A single militia guards it. Come around from the south, take him out, then grab the goods.

Move south to this alley.

Take out this enemy to the east.

Peek around the corner to take out militia across the street.

After healing yourself and resupplying, advance southwest to an alley that leads to the east-west road at G,1. Hold up in this alley while your team catches up to you. Before leaving its cover, take out militia in the buildings across the street to the south and southwest. When you are ready to move to the corner, turn and face the east as you peek. There is an enemy to the east. Drop him and move to the street corner to take out a second militia before returning to your alley.

Move west down the street.

A couple of militia hide in this alcove.

You have reached the convoy.

There are no more alleys, so move west along the road. Stay next to the buildings on the north side. Watch for snipers on the buildings to the south and southwest, and militia on the ground on both sides of the street. Use the binoculars to scout ahead, locating militia and taking them out before they can see you. Slowly and methodically make your way toward the convoy, which is waiting for you at B,2.

3. Get the convoy safely to the stadium.

Cross the street and move north of the convoy.

Move through the alleys to clear out militia waiting to ambush the convoy.

When you reach the convoy, it moves out. Grab more ammo and a first-aid kit marked on your GPS map in C,3. As the convoy heads east, move across the street so you are north of it. Move through the alleys of C,4 and D,4 to clear enemies waiting to ambush the convoy. Continue north to D,5 and provide fire support by engaging the militia to the north.

Cross the street toward this machinegun position to find a group of militia.

An RPG militia hides in this building.

Get your team to the stadium.

As the convoy passes by headed west, run across the road to E,6 and clear out this area. A number of militia, some with RPGs, hide in the building. Take them out before they fire on the convoy. Watch for snipers in the building to the north. After you clear this area, run for the convoy. Stay on its right side as it approaches the stadium. Follow the waypoints to the stadium to complete the mission. Stay on guard until the final APC enters the stadium. Militia will shoot RPGs and small arms fire at the convoy until the end.

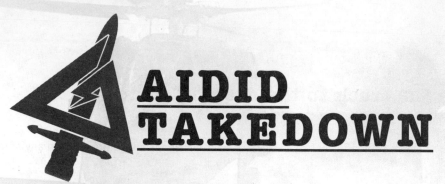

AIDID TAKEDOWN

BRIEFING

Date: 241545 July 96

Location: Mogadishu, Somalia

It's been nearly three years since Task Force Ranger pulled out of Mogadishu. The political situation there hasn't gotten much better. The clans are still fighting and there is no central government. Various groups claim to be the new government, but do not control a significant portion of Somalia. Mohammed Farah Aidid is still a major obstacle to stability in the area, but we may have an opportunity to change that.

One of the clans in Mogadishu has agreed to attack Aidid's militia as a cover for your operation. You'll insert via friendly ground transport and follow our informant to a safe house where they are digging a tunnel into Aidid's bunker. Infiltrate, find Aidid, and take him out. In all likelihood, it will appear as though he died in the fighting.

Remember, this is a black op. You can't be caught, and if you fail, we won't acknowledge that you were working for us. Good luck.

Summary of Mission

Somalia is still wracked with clan conflict. We've made an agreement to create an opportunity to take out Aidid with a clan that opposes him. This black op is designed to make it appear that Aidid died during clan fighting.

Suggested Loadout

Primary Weapon: MP5

Secondary Weapon: Shotgun

Accessory: Claymore

TACTICS

1. Ride the truck to the drop off point.

This mission is a bit different than any of the previous missions. It is the most difficult in the campaign, and you are completely on your own. Expect enemy militia to come at you from all directions. Don't think that because you cleared an area it is safe. Enemies will try to sneak up behind you throughout this mission.

Go along for the ride with the informant. Crouch or lie prone so you are not hit with as much enemy fire.

You begin the mission aboard a pickup truck, riding along with your informant. You must be very careful during the mission so that you do not shoot friendly militia. They look exactly like enemy militia, so you will need to be aware of the red cross that appears on friendlies when your crosshair rolls over them. While you are in the truck and facing to the rear, enemies will be primarily on your left side (the passenger side of the truck). Take out a few, but your main concern is to stay alive as you drive through a firefight.

2. Follow the informant to a nearby safe house; protect him from the enemy.

Duck behind the corner and peek around it to take out the militia following you from the street.

The truck eventually comes to a halt. Jump out and follow the informant down an alley to the north. About halfway down the alley, take a quick left and turn around so you are peeking around the corner toward the road where the truck stopped. Wait for three or four enemies to come down the alley toward you. Take them all out, then follow after the informant. He is north down the alley, then to the right. Stop before you reach the intersection. Position yourself in front of the informant and aim to the right side of the intersection. A couple of militia will come at you from the southeast. Drop them, then face north and peek to the right around the corner. Down the alley is a mounted machinegun. Quickly take out the enemy manning the gun, then move forward. Take a right at the intersection by the machinegun, then follow the alley around to the left so you face north again. A good technique for dealing with machinegunners is to lie prone just out of their sight, engage your scope, then use the lean feature. This will roll you to a stop with the enemy lined up directly in your crosshair for an easy head shot.

Clear out this courtyard quickly.

TIP *To help protect the informant from militia who might be coming up behind you, drop a Claymore mine along the east-west alley after you pass the machinegun. It will detonate and take out any militia coming that way.*

Next you need to get through an open courtyard area. Four militiamen are here. The informant will stay back in the alley until you clear the courtyard. Move in and clear out this area quickly. If you take too long, more enemies will come up from the alley behind you and attack the informant. If he dies, the mission is a failure. Therefore, if you need some more time to clear out the courtyard, head back for a bit to take out the enemies coming up from behind you.

These militiamen in the building are friendly.

Pick up the first-aid kit. You may need it by now.

After the courtyard has been cleared, the informant will lead you into a building. *Do not shoot anybody in the building!* They are friendly militia. At this point, you may need to turn on your night vision.

CAUTION *Shooting the friendly militia here will end the mission.*

A first-aid kit, which you could probably use by now, is in this room. The informant tells you that they have been building a tunnel and have nearly breached into Aidid's underground bunker. They just need you to finish it off.

3. Blow an entrance into Aidid's bunker.
4. Infiltrate Aidid's Underground Bunker.

Head down this ladder to the basement.

Throw a frag grenade down to gain access to Aidid's bunker.

In the corner of the room is a ladder leading down into the basement. Climb down the ladder and head west into a tunnel system. You eventually come to a flight of stairs leading down to a wall. Stay at the top of the stairs and throw a frag grenade to the bottom of the stairs. The grenade blasts open a passageway into Aidid's bunker. Descend the stairs and get ready for some enemy militia.

5. Eliminate the warlord Aidid.

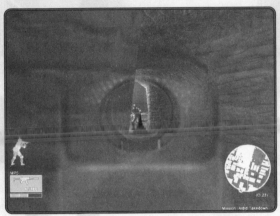

Fire down the tunnel at the militiamen coming toward you. Watch out for those who are just around the corner to your left.

Go for the enemies around the corner.

   Follow the tunnel around until you come to some crates on your right, where the tunnel turns to the left and an intersection. Hold here and aim down the tunnel to the south without exposing yourself to the tunnel leading off to the left. Use scope view and take out four militia that come down the tunnel directly ahead. Once you have neutralized them, peek to the right around the corner and take out the tangos in the hallway to your left, which leads east. There are several militia around the corner. Eliminate them all, then advance down this tunnel. Usually, one enemy patrols the tunnels and two are in a room off to the right. Although this tunnel branch dead-ends, make sure it is clear so these militia do not come up from behind you.

Throw a flashbang into this room off to the right...

...then rush in to take out the stunned militia.

Head back to the intersection and turn left. Follow it around until you hear some voices ahead. There is a room around the corner and to the left. Sidestep around the corner just enough so you can see into the corner of the room. Pull out a flashbang and throw it into the room. Switch back to the MP5. When the flashbang explodes, rush into the room and take down the two enemies while they are still stunned. Continue down the tunnel for a short bit. Halt when you come to an area where the tunnel widens.

Again you are clearing out the tunnel ahead at a distance while militiamen are close on your flank.

Peek around the corner to take out the enemies who man the machinegun.

Around the corner to the right are four militiamen and a mounted machinegun. However, they are not your first concern. Instead, face east toward where the tunnel continues on the other side of the wide area. Bring up scope view and wait. You will see militia walking back and forth past this opening. Take out the first militia, and a few more will come to the spot, allowing you to shoot them as well. Wait for about 30 seconds after you take down the last one to make sure no more are coming. Turn to face south, make sure your MP5 has a full clip, and peek to the left. If you cannot see anything just yet, while still peeking, sidestep to the left until you can just barely see the machinegun and an enemy. Take him out and any other militia who try to man the gun. Move in to clear out any remaining militia.

This is where you have to make a decision. Aidid is down the tunnel to the left. Lots of militiamen are to the right.

Throw a grenade at this wall.

First-aid kits and ammo boxes are inside.

With the wide area of the tunnel clear, now head to the passage on the east side. At this point, you can go either left or right. Aidid is to the left, so that is where you should go. Skip ahead to the next paragraph if you choose to go straight for Aidid. However, if you were to head to the right, you would come across lots of militia in several rooms. This way also branches again, making it possible for enemies from one branch to sneak up behind you while you clear the other branch. However, at the end of the branch on the right, you will come to a dead end with a rock wall covering what looks like a passageway at grid Q,22. If you look at your GPS map, you will see some green blips on the other side. Step back and throw a frag grenade at the wall. The explosion opens a new tunnel. Follow it to a couple of first-aid kits and a couple of ammo boxes. By this time, the section of the bunker should be clear, so head back to the intersection near the wide area with the machinegun at P,23. However, since you were here, some militiamen have moved the machinegun to this intersection in an effort to prevent you from reaching Aidid.

TIP *Before moving down the tunnel to the left, start placing some Claymore mines at the start of the tunnel to the right, and place the rest as you back into the tunnel leading to Aidid. This may not take out all four of the pursuing militia, but it should help.*

Drop the militia as they come around the corner of the tunnel after you.

While the detour lets you find a cool hidden room full of ammo and first-aid kits, there is no need to head down that tunnel unless you want to risk being killed. Therefore, you should take the left branch of the tunnel. Move forward into an area with some UN canisters and take out an enemy at the far east end. Then immediately turn around and face west. Four militia try to sneak up behind you. Take them all out.

Rush into the headquarters room after the enemies inside are stunned.

Aidid is the one in the striped shirt. Neutralize him.

Head east again. As you go around a corner to the right to face north, take out a militia directly ahead and behind some crates as well as his friend at a slight distance down the tunnel. With him out of the way, advance until you can see a room off to the left. Throw a flashbang inside. After it detonates, rush in and take down the militia guard. The third person, in the striped shirt, is Aidid. Drop everyone in this room before they recover from the stunning effects. On one side of the room are a first-aid kit and some more ammo. Pick them up and turn around to leave the room. Militia usually comes rushing in to see what is happening. Drop him and then take a left as you exit the room.

6. Exfiltrate yourself from the area.

Man the machinegun and take out any pursuers.

You come to some stairs before long. At least one enemy is at the top, and possibly another is heading down toward you. Take them both down, then climb up the stairs. Watch for another militia or two in the passage as you approach the top. When you reach the part of the tunnel that heads north, slow down. In a small room to the left is a militia manning a machinegun. Peek around the corner and take him out. Several enemies are hot on your tail, so quickly run up to the machinegun and take control. Aim out of the room and to the right. Mow down anyone that comes in from the left. Again, to make sure you got all of them, wait about 30 seconds after the last enemy falls until leaving the gun. As you exit the alcove, leave a Claymore mine facing down the tunnel toward the stairs.

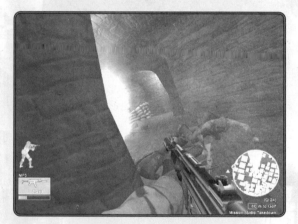

Peek around the corner to take out the machinegun position.

Continue down the tunnel to the north for a bit. When it goes south and then starts to turn to the east, be very careful. Around the corner to the left are several militia and a machinegun. Throw a frag grenade around the corner to take out some of the militia, then wait for others to come to you. When nothing more happens, peek around the corner and take out the enemy manning the machinegun. However, now that the way is clear, do not run forward; the enemy is expecting you to do that. Sidestep so you can peek around the corner facing north to take out a militia manning a second machinegun.

By this time, the tunnel area should be pretty much clear. Advance past the second machinegun and keep going until you reach a ladder. There is usually no one at the top, but it is a good idea to throw a flashbang anyway. Start to climb the ladder, waiting for the detonation before going to the top. If someone is there, drop the enemy while still stunned. Continue around a corner. A couple of militia are by the door to the building. Drop them and anyone who enters before moving to the door.

This ladder leads up to the ground level.

Hop into the back of this truck to complete the mission.

At the doorway, turn to face east, then peek around the corner. You should be able to take out two to three militiamen from this position. Once it looks clear, exit the building and head east toward the road. As you advance, check for an enemy around the corner of the building to your left. A militia hides in the small building near the road on your left side. Throw a frag grenade inside to take him out. As you approach the wall that runs next to the road, turn to face the north and sidestep to the right so you can line up a shot on an enemy patrolling along the road. With him down, hop into the back of the informant's white pickup truck to make your getaway. This not only completes the mission, but also the campaign.

MULTIPLAYER MISSIONS

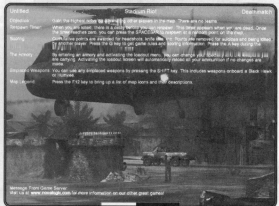

Although going up against a massive number of computer-controlled enemies can be a big challenge, facing off against human players offers an experience that the single-player campaign can not duplicate. Following in the tradition of previous *Delta Force* games, *Delta Force—Black Hawk Down* provides a great and exciting multiplayer experience on NovaWorld or a LAN.

Read the briefing while you wait for a multiplayer mission to begin. This tells you about your objectives and how you can score points.

Most multiplayer missions divide players into Blue and Red Teams and give them different objectives, which must be achieved to win the mission. Working with other players can be rewarding, especially when a plan comes together perfectly. However, the spontaneous and unscripted actions of your opponents can have you tearing out your hair as they get the drop on you by constantly changing their tactics. No matter what, the multiplayer aspect of *Delta Force—Black Hawk Down* is a completely different game, but uses the same weapons, equipment, and interface as the single-player campaign. Now that you are excited about taking on other players, let's see what type of missions you can play.

TYPES OF MULTIPLAYER MISSIONS

Deathmatch

Deathmatch is the common multiplayer game type found in nearly every game that offers multiplayer support. There are no teams and each player competes individually. Points are scored by eliminating the other players, and the one with the highest score—most kills when the timer expires is the winner.

In this type of game, it is a free-for-all. If you see somebody, shoot first. A successful Deathmatch player becomes the hunter and takes the initiative rather than just waiting around to be killed.

Team Deathmatch

This is similar to Deathmatch except that players are divided into two teams. Points are scored by taking out players of the opposing team. The team with the highest score at the end of the time limit is the winner. Once again, eliminating the enemy is the objective. However, this time you have other players to cover your back and help you take the battle to the enemy. The team that works together the best will almost always beat out a team of individuals—no matter how good they may be one-on-one.

Team King of the Hill

The objective is to occupy the Hot Zone until your team's timer reaches the target time first. You can reset the opposing team's timer to zero by eliminating all of its members from the Hot Zone.

The Hot Zone is marked on your GPS Map by a circle. When you are in the Hot Zone, you will see a display noting how far inside you are: 1% is right on the edge and 90% is near the center. As long as one player from a team is inside the circle, that team's timer continues to count. When a team's timer reaches the target time, that team wins. As soon as a team has no players inside the Hot Zone, that team's timer resets to zero. In addition to normal scoring, points are also awarded for time in the Hot Zone and for killing someone inside the Hot Zone.

Search and Destroy

This is a game requiring both teams to not only attack, but also defend an area. The objective is for each team to enter the opposing team's territory and destroy specific targets with satchel charges. The first team to destroy all enemy targets wins.

Place satchel charges next to your targets, then remotely detonate them to complete your objectives.

Each side has targets they must defend from the other side. These targets are marked on your GPS map by small squares of the opposing team's color. As you approach these targets, they are usually surrounded by a colored glow. Because CQB soldiers (Close Quarters Battle; see the following Combat Specialties section) are the only ones who carry satchel charges in multiplayer missions, make sure your team has plenty of this type of player to complete your objectives. While the CQB soldiers go on the attack, Snipers and Machinegunners can stay back to defend their team's targets from enemy destruction.

Attack and Defend

This is like a one-sided version of the previous type. Instead of both teams attacking and defending, one team is designated as the attacker while the other is the defender. The attacker must destroy a certain number of targets to win the game. The defender wins by preventing this from happening. This mission type lets each team concentrate on one role instead of having to balance their force between attacking and defending.

Capture the Flag

Return captured flags to your flag bay.

The objective of this mission type is to capture all the opposing team's flags and return them to your flag bay before the opposition captures all of your flags. To pick up a flag of the opposing team's color, run over it. A flag icon appears on your HUD to designate that you are a flag carrier. If a flag carrier is killed, the flag drops at the point of death. To return a friendly flag to your home base, run over it.

Flag Ball

In Flag Ball, there is one green flag for both teams to go after.

This mission type is kind of like a cross between football and capture the flag. There is only one green flag on the map. Everyone's GPS map shows a waypoint where the flag is located. When you pick up the flag, the new waypoint shows you the way to your team's flag bay. After you drop off the flag at the bay, it respawns somewhere else on the map. If the flag carrier is killed, the flag drops and remains at the site of the death for a limited amount of time before returning to its original location. The first team to drop off the flag at their bay a set number of times is the winner.

COMBAT SPECIALTIES

When playing on NovaWorld or on a LAN, you can choose a combat specialty for your character. Each specialty gives you advantages with certain weapon types, or gives you additional skills. Although you gain proficiencies, there may also be drawbacks to using weapons outside your character specialty. You can switch your specialty and weapon loadout during a game by entering an armory and changing your selections.

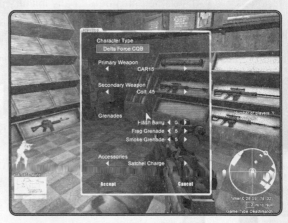

The types of weapons you can carry are limited depending on your military specialty.

Close Quarters Battle (CQB)

When the magazine is empty, the knives come out. This is when the CQB specialists shine. Their reach with a knife gives them great advantage when fighting in close. They are probably the most common specialty because they offer a good balance. CQB soldiers can carry the rifles and submachine gun, five of each grenade type, and satchel charges.

Sniper

The Sniper is trained to engage targets at great distances. They treat their guns, which have been tuned to their personal specifications, with great care. Their preferred weapons are the M21, M24, MCRT .300 Tactical, and Barrett sniper rifles. The number of grenades a Sniper can carry is limited. Snipers are the only specialty that can carry Claymore mines. Place these around your position to protect against enemies who try to sneak up on you while you are focused on a distant target through your scope.

Machinegunner

Controlling a weapon with a fire rate of over 600 rounds per minute requires skill, training, and muscle. Machinegunners prefer the weight and high magazine capability of the M249 SAW, M60E3, M240B, or emplaced machineguns, and are more accurate than their untrained teammates when using them. This specialty can carry a limited number of grenades, but makes up for this by using the AT4.

Medic

Medics are highly valued members of any military unit. In multiplayer games, Medics can save a character who has been shot and restore him or her to fighting form. When a player is shot, a Medic sees the injured character's friendly tag preceded with a countdown timer. If the Medic can reach that character and administer first aid before the timer expires, the character will survive.

To administer first aid, select the Medic Pack from your Inventory. Then, from a standstill at very close range, point your crosshairs at the injured character and left click your mouse. If you administer first aid in time, the injured player can respawn from that exact spot by pressing [space]. If the player's respawn timer expires before doing this, the player will respawn from his or her original spawn point.

Whereas all specialties receive points for killing enemies, Medics also earn points by saving teammates. As such, they are limited to only assault rifles without grenade launchers, a few grenades, and no explosives whatsoever. Although most players will want to take on the role of a specialty with more firepower, a good Medic or two can really make a difference on a team and help it to win.

ASPECTS OF A MULTIPLAYER MISSION

Multiplayer missions have a few unique aspects that don't appear in the single-player campaign. Let's take a look at them.

Progressive Spawn Points (PSPs)

Take control of as many PSPs as possible. As soon as a PSP starts changing color, take off. There is no need for you to stand out in the open waiting like a sitting duck.

A player killed during a multiplayer mission respawns at a team spawn point after a short wait. This team spawn point is often located at a distance from the action. However, some missions provide another means of spawning in different locations, often closer to the battle; these are Progressive Spawn Points (PSPs).

These positions are controlled by a specific team, and players of that team can respawn into the game at these locations after dying. At the beginning of a mission, all PSPs are neutral. Once captured, they the capturing team can use them.

To capture a PSP, walk up to it. If it is controlled by another team, it will immediately turn neutral, preventing any other players from that team from using it. It then changes to the capturing player's color. When capturing it, a timer bar appears. This does not represent how long it takes to capture the PSP. (Once the PSP changes to your color, it is yours.) The timer just represents the wait until your teammates can start using it. Therefore, there is no reason to wait around like a sitting duck while the PSP timer counts. Instead, take cover and continue fighting.

Armories

Armories are located throughout most multiplayer maps. They are represented on the map by a circle with an "A" in it. These can be trucks, bunkers, or a pile of weapons. At an armory, you can restock your ammo, change military specialty, and change weapons. Learn where they are in order to get more ammo or change specialties.

Armories are usually designated by this ordnance sign.

Scoring

If you access the mission briefing during the game, it usually includes a scoring chart.

Players can score points a number of ways during a multiplayer mission. Beyond points awarded for killing an opponent, earn additional points by completing objectives, killing with a knife or sniper rifle, and so forth. Conversely, penalties or negative points are assigned for killing yourself, other teammates, or by dying in combat. Scoring varies from mission to mission, so when you first begin a multiplayer mission, press G to bring up a mission briefing that explains what your team must do to win and how many points are awarded for various actions.

Vehicles

Man the machinegun on a Humvee as it patrols the town.

Lie prone in the Black Hawk and shoot through the door.

In most multiplayer missions, you have the opportunity to use vehicles. Although you do not actually get to drive or fly them, you can ride on them and use their mounted weapons. There may be one or two types of vehicles available.

Humvees drive on their own. You can hop aboard and use a machinegun as you move through the map. Black Hawk helicopters also are available. They start from landing zones (LZs) marked with an "H" on the map. Once a player climbs aboard, the helicopter waits a short amount of time, then takes off and flies a circuit around the map. Eventually, it will return to the original LZ or another one somewhere else on the map. Not only can players use the two miniguns to mow down enemies below, but the Black Hawk also serves as a great Sniper perch. Though the platform is in constant motion, a good sniper can lie prone in the door of the chopper and take out targets below.

Enemies cannot destroy the Humvees or Black Hawks, but they can kill players riding in them.

TACTICS FOR MULTIPLAYER MISSIONS

You can use the same tactics for multiplayer missions that you used in the single-player game. Remember to look for and use cover and concealment as much as possible.

Communications

A critical component of team play is communication with your teammates. By pressing [Y], you can open a text box and type in a message. When you press [enter], your message is only sent to players on your team. If you open the text box by pressing [T], you send a global message to all players.

Emotes

Another cool feature that *Delta Force—Black Hawk Down* offers is emotes—nonverbal actions that communicate an order or idea to your teammates. To issue an emote, press [F9]. This opens a window listing the nine different emotes you can give. Press a key to cause your character to perform an action seen by other players.

Emotes are a quick and silent way to communicate with your team.

Emote Commands

Key	Action
1	Salute
2	Go Forward
3	Take Cover
4	Let's Go
5	Come this Way
6	Celebration 1
7	Celebration 2
8	Play Dead
9	Flip/ Do Pirouettes

Teamwork

Teamwork is among the most important tactics in *Delta Force—Black Hawk Down*. If you have enough players, pair them or create even larger teams. Two people see twice as much as one and can accomplish different tasks, making the team more effective.

TIP *Ideally, a team contains different specialists, including a Machinegunner, Medic, and CQB. Snipers are usually better off operating alone or with one other teammate who can provide cover and protection as the Sniper sets up and takes shots at the enemy.*

A team comprising multiple operatives is useful for clearing rooms. One operative covers the doorway, another tosses a frag grenade or flashbang inside, and the rest cover the area around the team. All operatives then run through the doorway and spread out left and right. This prevents anyone from being shot in the back because he or she looked left when the enemy was right. (Practice helps teams develop the precise timing that such tactics require.) Other players can help prevent surprises from the rear.

Think about spacing between team members. Stay close enough to support one another, but not so close that a single automatic burst would take out your whole team. Space team members far enough apart so that they can support one another without allowing a single grenade to kill them all.

Every team needs a leader. In this game, you lead from the front, so the leader is usually the point man. In large games, where each side has multiple teams, an overall commander coordinates the teams' actions.

Movement

Outdoors, it's important to spread out and cover every angle. Open windows, doors, corners, balconies—any place an enemy could hide—represent points of threat. Watch them. Spreading out in the open provides the enemy with fewer targets.

Indoors, keep your teammates close together so they don't lose their way. If you become lost, everyone behind you is lost. Confusion sets in, and you usually die. If you're in position 2, keep the point man in sight. If you're in position 4, keep the position 3 operative in sight. However, staying close to the person ahead of you can have disadvantages; enemy frag grenades or automatic fire will wipe out a bunched up team.

When you must pass through a choke point, do so as quickly as possible. The same goes for open areas. If you can't cover all angles of threat, move as fast as you can to minimize the chance that the enemy will hit you.

If you must climb stairs, face toward where the enemy could be. This may mean going up sideways or even backward. Stairs can be dangerous choke points.

Fire Discipline

Because a single shot often kills, and a three-round burst nearly always does, avoid using full-automatic fire. Firing while moving is highly inaccurate. If you miss a target, you alert the enemy to your presence and give them the opportunity to fire back. As a general rule, stop, drop, and fire! This will increase your accuracy and minimize your chance of being detected if you miss.

There are some instances where full-automatic fire and movement are acceptable. If you must get through a choke point or a large open area, running and firing wildly at the enemy may force them to keep their heads down and prevent them from accurately firing at you.

Attacking

There are several different ways to attack the enemy. In most cases, advance slowly and carefully as a team, using good fire discipline and covering each other. However, there are also times when rushing the enemy has benefits.

The best way to advance is by using "bound and overwatch." This tactic divides a team into two parts. While one advances, the other covers it. When the first gets to some cover, it halts and covers the second group as it advances. Practice this tactic so everyone on your team understands his or her role.

Defending

Defending a position entails setting up firing positions, ambushes, and Snipers. This takes time, so at the start of a mission, each player should assume a defensive position in case the enemy immediately rushes your position.

For firing positions, choose locations with cover and far from an entrance. This increases your ability to survive grenade attacks and makes it harder for the enemy to shoot you.

Locate choke points and set up your defenses near them. It's hard to defend a large area, so concentrate on narrow spots through which the enemy must advance. Use satchel charges or a Claymore to blast a hole in an enemy's attack. Grenades also come in handy.

FIFTEEN KEY TIPS AND HINTS FOR MULTIPLAYER MISSIONS

1. **Move decisively and with purpose! You're the hunter, so attack your enemy with confidence. If you move like a victim, you'll soon be one.**

2. **Put your opponent under duress—if you see your enemy, open fire! With rounds flying, the enemy will panic, giving you (or preferably your partner) the chance to take a good kill shot.**

3. **Teamwork! Trust your teammates to cover their zones and do their jobs. Just watching a locked door far from the action can save your whole team from being wiped out from behind.**

4. **Never assume a room is cleared simply because you've already been in there.**

5. **Remember: short, controlled bursts. It doesn't matter how many rounds you fire—just where they land.**

6. **Never put your back to an open window or door.**

7. **As a team, secure all entries into your location as quickly as possible. Do this every time you enter a new room during an advance so the enemy doesn't surprise you.**

8. Peek around corners before rounding them! This will save your life again and again. It's harder to hit half a head than it is to hit half a body.

9. If your teammates' bodies were piled near a window or door in real life, would you go to see what killed them? Why do it in the game?

10. Along the same lines, if you peek around a corner and the enemy nearly shoots your head off, don't stick your head around again. It's better to let them think you're there, then flank them or get some teammates and set up an ambush.

11. Teamwork is essential. Find each team member's special skill or ability and work on those strengths. For example, if you have quick, accurate shots among your players, cast them as Snipers and develop tactics to take advantage of their skills. They can always move to a high spot or provide cover for your assaulting team members.

12. When you must move across an enemy-covered area, throw smoke grenades and lay down plenty of scattered rounds where you think they're hiding as part of your team moves. They'll be less likely to poke their guns around the corner.

13. Don't discount stealth. More often than not, it's the sneaky operative who gets the kill.

14. Develop standard operating procedures and break-contact drills. That way, everyone will know what to do when the bullets start flying. Often, the best tactic is to get out of there (break contact) and set up an ambush somewhere else on *your* terms.

15. When patrolling, stay in formation. Move only as fast as your slowest operative—usually your rear guard. (It should be your point man if he wants to live a long time.)